# The New ABC's of Life for Children and Adults:

Short Stories, Essays, and Poems Promoting Christian Concepts

# The New ABC's of Life for Children and Adults:

## Short Stories, Essays, and Poems Promoting Christian Concepts

Pamela K. Orgeron, M.A., Ed.S., BCCC, ACLC

ABC's Ministries
Madison, TN 37115

*The New ABC's of Life for Children and Adults: Short Stories, Essays, and Poems Promoting Christian Concepts*
Copyright © 2016 by Pamela K. Orgeron. All rights reserved.

Library of Congress Control Number: Pending
ISBN PB 978-0-692-63950-4

Printed in the United States of America

First Edition
*The ABC's of Life for Children and Adults: Short Stories, Essays, and Poems Promoting Christian Concepts*
Copyright © 2003 by Pamela K. Owens

Library of Congress Control Number: Pending
ISBN PB 1-594670-08-0; HC 1-594670-09-9

No part of this publication may be reproduced or transmitted in any form or by any means without written permission of the publisher.

Unless otherwise indicated, Bible quotations are taken from *Spirit-Filled Life Bible. New King James Version.* Copyright © 1991 by Thomas Nelson.

# Dedication

First, I dedicate this book to Jesus Christ,
The Lord and Savior. Without
Him, completing both editions of this book
would have been impossible.

Additionally, I dedicate this book to my parents,
Harry Marvin and Patricia Ann Owens,
of Russell, KY and my husband,
Milton Joseph Orgeron.

I also write this book in memory of
my late paternal grandmother,
Earl Smith Owens,
who first shared
The Gospel with me and
who always encouraged me
towards academic pursuits.

Also in loving memory of
Aunt Neva Joy Conley (Sturgill)
Uncle Wilburn Garland Sturgill
Uncle Delmar Glen Sturgill
Uncle Harold Joe Sturgill,
Cousin Charles "Chuck" Sturgill
Cousin Glen Randall Sturgill
Great Aunt Ida Smith Gillum
Great Aunt Phoebe Smith Adams (Audie)
Cousin D. V. "Gill" Gillum ("Tiny")
Cousin Hermal V. Adkins

# Good-bye, "Pop"!
# I'll meet you in Glory!

*Photo taken June 11, 1983*

**Elder Harry M. Owens, 1936-2016**

My father, Elder Harry Marvin Owens, 79, of Russell, loving husband, father, grandfather and great-grandfather, went home to his Lord and Savior Wednesday, Feb. 17, 2016, at Oakmont Manor in Flatwoods, Kentucky following an extended illness.

Harry was born June 11, 1936, in Ashland, Kentucky, a son of the late Harry H. and Earl Smith Owens.

He was ordained as a United Baptist minister in 1993, being saved in 1963, and was a member of Martha United Baptist Church, Raceland, Kentucky. Harry also retired as an electrician at AK Steel Corp. in Ashland, Kentucky after 40 years of service.

# Contents

***ABC*'s TO SUCCESSFUL LIVING** ..........................XIII

**Preface** ..................................................................XV

**Introduction** ………………………………………XVII

### Section I
### Fiction for the Children

Paying Attention Pays Off ………………………………..3

Respect Reaps Rewards ………………………………..7

Honesty Wins a Friend ………………………………..12

A Child's Prayer ………………………………………16

Building Trust Takes Time ………………………………..21

Christian Takes Time to Touch a Life ……………………...27

Patience's Prayers Prevent Peril ……………………………33

Lying Lips Lose ……………………………………38

Attitudes of Gratitude ………………………………..44

A Forever Family ………………………………………..50

Sharing Jilts Jealousy ……………………………………55

## Section II
## Lessons Learned from Life's Realities

Handicapped? You Decide! ............................................................**65**

Yes, God Does Provide ..................................................**70**

God Knows Best .........................................................**75**

Put Unjust Bias to Death ................................................**80**

Ground Gossip ..........................................................**85**

Wipe out Worry .........................................................**90**

Cease Slothfulness .....................................................**95**

Give Generously .......................................................**100**

Fail not to Forgive ....................................................**106**

More Than a Grandmother ................................................**111**

A Marriage Made in Heaven ..............................................**114**
*Milton J. and Pamela K. Orgeron*

Maintaining Christian Character Costs...................................**118**

## Section III
## Moments from the Heart

### Complete Works of Pamela K. Owens, Volume One © 1993

Unchanging Love ....................................**126**

No Better Friend ...................................**128**

Turned Around .................................................. 130

Let the Son Shine ............................................. 132

Channel of Blessings ....................................... 134

Trials with Triumph ......................................... 135

Bright and Morning Star .................................. 136

Heaven's Highway ........................................... 138

In the Name of Jesus ....................................... 139

Bless Us to be a Blessing ................................. 140

### **Tributes to Loved Ones**

Harry and Earl Smith Owens ............................ 142

Dave and Emma Whitley Sturgill .................... 144
*Patricia Sturgill Owens*

Helen Sturgill Moore and Jim Sturgill ............. 146
*Patricia Sturgill Owens*

Helen Sturgill Moore ....................................... 148

Emma Moore McGlone ................................... 150

John William Sturgill ...................................... 152

Forty One Years, *Harry Marvin Owens* ............... 154

The King's Highway, *Harry Marvin Owens* ........ 156

From Darkness to Light, *Patricia Sturgill Owens* ..... 157

Such Precious Moments, *Patricia Sturgill Owens* ......................**158**

Peaceful Shores, *Harry Marvin Owens*...............................**159**

Against the Odds: The Author's Personal Testimony ..............**160**

Twelve Years Later: A New Perspective ....................................**163**

Final Reflections and Acknowledgements ...........................**165**

## *ABC*'s TO SUCCESSFUL LIVING

A---BE AUTHENTIC
B---BE a BLESSING to others
C---BE a person of CHARACTER
D---BE DECISIVE
E---BE EAGER to learn
F---BE FRUITFUL
G---BE GENEROUS
H---BE HOLY
I---BE IMPECCABLE
J---BE JOYFUL
K---BE KINDHEARTED
L---BE a LISTENER
M---BE MATURE in CHRIST
N---BE NURTURANT
O---BE OBSERVANT
P---BE PATIENT
Q---BE QUICK-THINKING
R---BE REASONABLE
S---BE SLOW to SPEAK
T---BE THANKFUL
U---BE UNDEMANDING
V---BE VERSATILE
W---BE WELL-ORGANIZED
X---BE a positive eXample to others
Y---BE YIELDING to God
Z---BE ZEALOUS

# Preface

The *ABC's of Life for Children and Adults: Short Stories, Essays, and Poems Promoting Christian Concepts* is a book I wrote over twelve years ago depicting Biblical principles and morals of life that society seemed to have lost. By writing the book, I hoped to teach children, and remind adults about values such as honesty, decency and a strong work ethic by emphasizing their importance throughout the book.

*ABC*s used in the title is an acronym for: Abolishing apathetic attitudes; Building Biblical behavior patterns; and, Choosing Christ-like character. I believed that through reminding ourselves and teaching our children healthy attitudes and behavior Christians could make a difference that would result in worldwide revival. I thought, *Christ-like character needs to be displayed and encouraged by Christians of all denominations.*

The *ABC's of Life for Children and Adults* was divided into three sections: 1. "Fiction for the Children"; 2. Nonfiction material, "Lessons Learned from Life's Realities", developed from experiences in my life, or the lives of individuals influential in my life; and, 3. "Moments from the Heart", which contained the lyrics of a collection of songs I wrote. In addition, this section included poetry written by either my father or me.

The *ABC's of Life for Children and Adults* concluded with a list of what I entitled *ABC*s TO SUCCESSFUL LIVING. The list included positive qualities, which I hoped everyone reading the earlier edition of this book would strive to possess. I gave credit for the existence of the book to God. Any good that came from that book should be given to the glory of God. My primary purpose of writing *The ABC's of Life for Children and Adults* was to glorify the Lord and Savior, Jesus Christ.

# Introduction

This book is a revised and expanded edition of the book *The ABC's of Life for Children and Adults: Short Stories, Essays, and Poems Promoting Christian Concepts*. To be honest, I did not practice what I preached when I published the first edition. In the initial stages of writing the earlier book, I had planned to include poems written by both my father and my mother. Without telling them I pulled the poems before the final editing due to tight finances and "unfinished business" internally. This was wrong of me and really hurt both my father and mother. I did apologize to them years ago. You have heard people use the expression, "putting feet to your prayers". Well, I believe the opportunity to write and publish this second edition to my book (which really belongs to God) is God allowing me to put feet to my apology to right the wrong I did in 2003. I love you, Dad and Mom! Yes, I know I have egg on my face now.

In addition to the omitted poems written earlier by either my father or my mother, The *New ABC's of Life for Children and Adults* includes "Questions for Reflection" at the end of each fiction and non-fiction story. Additionally, I added additional Scripture references and their application at the end of each fiction story for children. These additions were prompted by the number of parents who told me they had used the earlier version of this book as a devotional guide with their children. My prayer is that these new chapter tools will help even more parents in teaching their children biblically based morals. Furthermore, I made revisions in the book chapters and included new stories not previously published.

The ABCs TO SUCCESSFUL LIVING, which concluded the earlier edition, has been moved to the front of this book. This change is intended to give more relevance to the positive qualities I believe each of us individuals should strive to develop as part of our character.

In spite of my earlier trespass against my parents, God has blessed me since I published The *ABC's of Life for Children and Adults*. He has blessed me with personal, academic, and professional achievements above and beyond what I expected. Personally, the Lord sent me a wonderful, godly husband. Academically, I have been blessed to complete, in addition to the previously received Master of Arts degree, an Education Specialist degree in 2009, also from Morehead State University, Morehead, KY. Professionally, I have added to my credentials Board Certified Christian Counselor (BCCC), Advanced Christian Life Coach (ACLC) and General Partner in ABC's Ministries.

On the other hand, while I have seen progress personally, I see a much deeper decline overall in the moral compass of the United States of America and around the world since I published *The ABC's of Life for Children and Adults*. Look at the increasing number of Christians persecuted for their faith, the continued killing of unborn babies, and the attempts to redefine God-ordained marriage between one man and one woman. With these events now I have an even greater and more urgent desire to share the themes of Abolishing apathetic attitudes; Building Biblical behavior patterns; and, Choosing Christ-like character depicted throughout the contents of both editions of the book. I believe that without revival now among the churches and a fresh spiritual awakening among lost souls our nation is doomed for destruction like we have never seen before.

Revival and spiritual awakening must begin with prayer and repentance. I concur with the prophecy given by Anne Graham Lotz (See citation below.). Lotz (2016) wrote:

> I have been repeatedly warned in my spirit that the enemy is advancing. It's something that *I know*. And I feel compelled, like Jehoshaphat, to lead God's people also in a desperate prayer for help before we plunge past the point of no return into the abyss of God's judgment.

The above words by Lotz are my sentiments too. However, my sentiments are broader in scope. Like Lotz, I believe prayer and repentance (changing our minds to agree with God that we have sinned and turning from that sin) are the foundation for revival and spiritual awakening. Additionally, I believe Christians need to live a Holy Spirit led life. By Christians reflecting Christ through living a Holy Spirit led life, my hope and prayer is that the lost will see and want the joy and peace in us that only comes through the gift of salvation.

With the above circumstances, God birthed *The New ABC's of Life for Children and Adults: Short Stories, Essays, and Poems Promoting Christian Concepts* in my heart. I hope and pray that others are as inspired by reading this new edition as I have been redoing the book. Blessings always to everyone!

Citation: Lotz, Anne Graham (2016, January). Anne Graham Lotz Gives Prophetic Warning About 2016. Charisma Magazine. Retrieved January 15, 2016 online from http://www.charismanews.com/opinion/54206-anne-graham-lotz-gives-prophetic-warning-about-2016.

- 1 -

# Fiction for
# The Children

## Psalm 23

1 A Psalm of David. The Lord is my shepherd; I shall not want.
2 He makes me to lie down in green pastures; He leads me beside the still waters.
3 He restores my soul; He leads me in the paths of righteousness For His name's sake.
4 Yea, though I walk through the valley of the shadow of death, I will fear no evil; For You are with me; Your rod and Your staff, they comfort me
5 You prepare a table before me in the presence of my enemies; You anoint my head with oil; My cup runs over.
6 Surely goodness and mercy shall follow me All the days of my life; And I will dwell in the house of the Lord Forever.

# Paying Attention Pays Off

Headed home after school, 10 year old Michaela and her seven year old brother Christopher were a short distance from their family's farm where they lived, when they heard the county's tornado warning siren. Knowing the life-threatening danger of a tornado, Michaela yelled to Christopher, "Run Chris! We have to get to the storm cellar in the barn."

Grabbing Chris's hand, Michaela pulled her brother towards the barn, as she screamed at her family's pet dog, and cat, "Come on, Lady! Run, Patches!" Lady and Patches followed pursuit having learned through obedience training to obey the children's commands.

"Look, Chris!" Michaela said to her brother. "Dad's chickens are following us. They must be afraid of the storm."

As the group neared the barn, Michaela could see her father, Jeremy, standing in the doorway frowning with a red face and wrinkled forehead. When Jeremy spotted the children running towards the barn, he raised his arms, shouting, "Thank God! You are here!"

Upon reaching the inside of the barn, Michaela recalled seeing Widow Grace working in her garden as the children passed her home half a mile away. "Wait, Dad! Widow Grace!!", Michaela shrieked. Widow Grace had become like a mother to Michaela. Michaela's mother had died of cancer a few months after Chris's birth.

"There is no time!", Jeremy exclaimed as he opened the cellar door. "Get in now!"

Descending the cellar steps, Michaela whispered a prayer, "Thank You, God, for the safety of this storm cellar. Please, God, keep Widow Grace safe."

Inside the cellar, Michaela grabbed her well-worn Bible and a flashlight that she kept stored there. Michaela loved studying God's Word. She often came to the cellar's solitude to read her Bible, to think and to pray.

While Jeremy and Chris turned their battery-powered radio to the local station for weather details, Michaela opened her Bible and turned on the flashlight. The pages opened to Psalm 23. "The Lord is my shepherd . . . ," she read. *How comforting*, she thought.

Within the hour the local radio station announcer reported that the storm system had passed. A small tornado had moved through town, but to their knowledge, there was no extensive damage or lives lost. The danger subsided with minor damage. Moments later the Marshall family left the cellar to survey the storm's damage. The instant Michaela reached ground level in the barn, she took off on her bicycle stored in the barn as she yelled back, "I'm going to check on Widow Grace. Come on, Lady!"

With Lady following her, Michaela rode swiftly to the widow's flower garden where the children had spotted her last. Michaela knew Widow Grace wouldn't have heard the storm's warning signal with her almost total hearing loss. Michaela feared what she might find.

Within minutes Michaela reached the edge of the widow's garden. Widow Grace laid among wet red roses with blood trickling down her forehead. Tears welled in Michaela's eyes. *I have to stay calm so I can get help*, she thought. Michaela checked to see if she could awaken the widow. Alas! The widow was out cold, but breathing.

"The telephone . . . I have to get inside her house," Michaela whispered to herself. She ran to find the kitchen door ajar. "Now, please let the telephone work," Michaela prayed aloud as she ran inside to call 911.

"County sheriff's office. Pearl speaking. Do you have an emergency?"

"Yes, Pearl. This is Michaela Marshall. Widow Grace was hurt in the storm. Please send help to her home."

"I'll send someone right away."

After hanging up the telephone, Michaela found clean towels. She wrapped ice in one that she placed on the widow's head to stop the bleeding. Both her father and Widow Grace had wrapped ice in clean cloths many times to apply to bleeding cuts.

"God, please let this stop her bleeding," Michaela prayed.

Before help arrived, the bleeding stopped. The widow awoke wanting to go inside. However, Michaela insisted that she remain still. Glancing away but still holding ice on the widow's head, Michaela glimpsed Lady running towards home.

Lady's loud barking as she approached the farm interrupted Chris and Jeremy cleaning up debris. "Where's Michaela, Lady?" Chris said.

"Chris, something must be wrong for Lady to be barking like that. Come on, Son. Let's find your sister." Father and son followed Lady to Widow Grace's where other help also had arrived.

The sheriff transported Widow Grace to the County Hospital where she was found to have numerous cuts and bruises and a broken hip along with the more serious cut on her forehead. She spent two weeks in the hospital before being released into the care of the Marshall family. After living with the Marshall family for six months, Widow Grace returned to her farm where Chris and Jeremy visited her every day after school.

## Questions for Reflection

1. Do you think Mr. Marshall should have allowed Michaela to return to check on Widow Grace when she asked? Why or why not?
2. Michaela prayed for Widow Grace when she thought she might be in trouble. Have you ever prayed for someone in a similar situation?
3. Why did Michaela want to make sure Widow Grace was okay?
4. The Marshall family did more for Widow Grace than most people would expect anyone to do in today's society. How do you think this made Widow Grace feel?
5. How did Michaela reflect Christ in her life?
6. Who was your favorite character in the story? Why?
7. Do you know what to do if you are ever in a bad storm like a tornado?

**The following Scriptures are other Bible verses and their application to "Paying Attention Pays Off":**

| Scripture Reference: | Application: |
|---|---|
| Isaiah 46:4 | God took care of Widow Grace. |
| James 1:27 | The Marshall family helped Widow Grace. |
| Psalm 46 | Michaela turned to God in the storm. |

## **Respect Reaps Rewards**

"Janice, your grandparents called. They're going to be here next Friday to spend the night." Eleven year old Janice sat across the dinner table from her mother eating a drumstick with macaroni and cheese. "You'll need to plan on being home."

"Oh, no, Mom! Don't you remember? That's the night I'm helping Mrs. Riptide host Natalie's surprise birthday party. You know Natalie is my best friend."

"Well, Janice, you know Granny and Pappy don't get to see you but a couple of times a year. Out of respect for them, I think you need to be home."

"I know, Mom. But, Natalie also is my best friend, and I did promise her mother I'd help. What am I going to do?"

"Looks like you have a decision to make. Think about what you want to do. Ask God for guidance," her mother said.

After dinner Janice went to lay across her king-sized bed. She stared at the blue-green of the pond outside her window beyond the patio and her swing set. She thought about the decision her mother asked her to make.

"I can't change the day of Natalie's birthday," Janice whispered to herself. "Maybe Granny and Pappy can come another weekend. I know. I'll go ask Mom to ask them."

"Mom, may we talk? I need to ask you something," Janice said to her mother, standing over the kitchen sink washing dishes.

"Sure, Janice, sit down at the table while I finish cleaning out the sink."

"Mom, I've been thinking about next Friday night's situation. I was wondering whether Granny and Pappy could plan their visit another weekend. You know how much I'd hate missing Natalie's birthday celebration. Would you please talk to them for me?"

"Sure, Janice, I'll e-mail Pappy from work tomorrow. I'll let you know his reply tomorrow evening."

After school the next day Janice ran home, as she prayed, "Lord, please let Granny and Pappy come another weekend. You know I promised I'd help Natalie's mother with the surprise birthday party."

At home Janice found her mother in the kitchen.

"Hi, Mom. What are you cooking?" Janice laid her school books on the counter.

"Meatloaf. Did you have a good day at school?" her mother replied as she added chopped onions to the meat mixture.

"School was okay. But I kept thinking about Natalie's birthday. Did you e-mail Pappy?"

"Yes, Janice. I received Pappy's reply before I clocked out at noon. He said the reason they are coming next weekend is to attend Granny's 50-year high school class reunion Saturday. Granny doesn't want to miss that because her former classmates plan to make this year's reunion their last one. I hope you understand. Otherwise, Pappy said they'd come another weekend, for your sake. With the present circumstances, you need to be home to visit with your grandparents."

"Okay, Mom. Let me talk to Natalie's mother."

"Mrs. Riptide? This is Janice. Is Natalie around, or can you talk now?"

"Hi, Janice. Natalie is in her room doing her homework. I can talk. I look forward to your helping me host Natalie's party."

"That's why I called. I don't think I can help now. My grandparents are coming into town for my grandmother's class reunion Saturday. Mom wants me home Friday night."

"Oh, no, Janice. I was counting on you to help me pull off the surprise element of Natalie's party. I guess I can talk to Natalie's grandmother again to see if she'll change her mind. I hope you can stop by for a few minutes, at least, Friday night. Natalie thinks highly of you. She considers you her best friend."

"Natalie is my best friend also. I have to hang up now. Will you let me know what Natalie's grandmother says?"

"Yes, Janice. I'll call you back. Bye now."

"Janice, the telephone is for you," her mother yelled from downstairs.

"Thanks, Mom. I'll use the telephone upstairs."

"Hello, this is Janice."

"Hi, Janice. This is Mrs. Riptide. You won't believe what I learned from Natalie's grandmother. Her grandmother, my husband's mother, said she declined my initial invitation to help me because she was busy making last minute preparations for her 50-year class reunion Saturday. I didn't know about that."

"You're kidding! You mean Natalie's grandmother and my grandmother went to school together?! How cool!"

"Yes, Janice. They were best friends for several years."

"Hey, I know! Why don't we move Natalie's party to our house? Then we could surprise both Natalie and my grandmother. Of course, I'll have to ask Mom."

"Mom, we need to talk," Janice said to her mother. "You won't believe this . . . but, Granny and Natalie's grandmother were friends in school. May we have Natalie's party here? Then we'd be having a double celebration: Natalie's surprise party and surprising Granny with seeing an old friend sooner than expected. Natalie's mother liked the idea. Please, can we?"

"That sounds fine to me. Looks like you won't have to disappoint either Natalie and her mother, or Granny and Pappy."

The rest of the week went by quickly. Friday arrived.

That morning Natalie's mother asked her whether she would like to go skating for her birthday. She also told her she would pay for Janice to go along. At school when Natalie asked Janice to go skating, she acted surprised and said she would go but that someone would have to give her a ride to the skating rink. After school Janice rushed home excited to help her mother make final preparations for the surprise reunion for the two grandmothers and for her friend's surprise birthday party.

Meanwhile, at Natalie's house, "Grandma, Mom said she had to go to the store," Natalie said. "She asked that you take me over to pick up Janice for us to go skating later. I think Mom planned for her to eat with us too."

Grandma Riptide already knew about the plans for her granddaughter's surprise birthday party. She agreed to drive her to Janice's house where unknowingly she too had a surprise.

"Why, for mercy's sake," Grandma Riptide said when she thought she recognized her old school friend standing in the door way. "Is that you, Bessie?"

"Yes, Jenny, it's me. Where has the time gone? We haven't seen each other in almost fifty years." Both grandmothers cried tears of joy at their surprise reunion.

Natalie, standing in the background with all her school and church friends, said, "This is the best birthday ever! I want to thank everyone for coming."

## Questions for Reflection

1. Why did Janice feel conflicted over the decision she had to make?
2. Why do you think Janice's mother preferred she be at home Friday night instead of at Natalie's house?
3. What did Janice's mother tell her to do about the conflicting schedules? What would you have done?
4. How did Janice's mother reflect Christ in her life?
5. Mrs. Riptide and Janice lied to Natalie about what they planned to do Friday evening for her birthday. Is lying ever okay?
6. What could Mrs. Riptide and Janice have done differently to avoid lying? What would you have done?
7. Respect and honesty both are important elements in this story. How so?

---

**The following Scriptures are other Bible verses and how they apply to "Respect Reaps Rewards":**

| Scripture Reference: | Application: |
| --- | --- |
| Proverbs 8:6-8; 12:22; Ephesians 4:25 | Always be honest. |
| Colossians 3:21; Ephesians 6:4 | Janice's mother's parenting |
| Galatians 5:13-14 | Janice helping Mrs. Riptide |

## Honesty Wins a Friend

"Class, Robert lost $20 on the playground before school this morning," Mrs. Layman said. "If anyone finds his money, would you please bring the money to me?"

"Big deal," Marvin heard the boy sitting behind him whisper in his ear. "If I find any money, I'm keeping it. Robert's parents are rich. Twenty dollars to him is like a penny to us."

"Well, be quiet," Marvin whispered back. "You'll get me in trouble." Marvin turned his attention to Mrs. Layman writing the new spelling words for that week on the chalk board.

"Did I hear someone say something?" Mrs. Layman turned to face the class. No one responded.

"If I hear anymore talking, the whole class will stay inside for recess. Now let's have our spelling bee on last week's words."

Marvin, the boy who sat behind him, and one of the girls in the class were the last three students standing in the spelling bee whenever the recess bell rang.

"We'll finish the spelling bee after recess." Mrs. Layman dismissed the class.

"I'm going outside to play on the monkey bars," Marvin said. The rest of the children were already exiting the classroom.

Outside on the playground most of the children were swinging or riding the merry-go-round. A few of the boys were organizing a game of softball. But, Marvin headed for the monkey bars. He loved to climb.

"Marvin, be careful climbing," Mrs. Layman yelled. "I don't want any accidents!"

"Okay, Mrs. Layman!" Marvin reached for the highest bar. "I won't fall," he said as he hung upside down swinging his body. *I could do this all day*, he thought. *But, then I wouldn't have the fun of beating the other kids at the spelling bee.*

As Marvin hung upside down he noticed a piece of paper laying on the ground. *What's that?* he thought. *I'll have to see if that's the money Robert lost.*

While Marvin was climbing to the ground, the boy who sat behind him in class approached. *What's he want*, Marvin thought.

As Marvin neared the ground, he realized the piece of paper he spotted below him was a twenty dollar bill.

"Hey, there's Robert's money," Marvin said without thinking.

"Where?" the boy approaching said. Marvin pointed to the bill. "Hey, Marv, since you spotted the money first, how about if we split the money? Robert isn't hurting for cash."

"No." Marvin grabbed the $20. "Giving the money back is the right thing to do."

The bell rang ending recess. Mrs. Layman motioned for all the children to come inside. Marvin ran towards her with the money in his hand. "Mrs. Layman! Mrs. Layman, I found Robert's money."

"Hey, Marvin, you found my money!" Marvin heard Robert yell from behind him.

"Yes, your money was under the monkey bars. I was about to give the money to Mrs. Layman. Since you're here, I'll return the money to you."

"Thanks, Marvin." Marvin handed Robert the $20. "Hey, Marv, would you like to go with me to the soda shop across the street during lunch? I'll buy you a sandwich and a soda as a reward."

"Gee, thanks, Robert," Marvin said as the two boys continued walking towards the school building. "That other boy wanted to keep the cash. I couldn't do that, even though you and I've never been close friends."

"That could change, Marvin," Robert patted him on the shoulder as they walked. "I appreciate your honesty."

"I always thought you were a snob," Marvin said. "However, now that we're talking, you don't seem that way. I'm sorry I misjudged you."

"That's okay, Marvin. With my parents the wealthiest family in town, a lot of people assume that I'm a snob. I'm quiet-natured because I don't have any brothers and sisters."

"Really! I also am an only child; so, I can understand!"

"Well, Marv, it looks like we both have found a new friend," Robert said. The two boys entered the classroom. "Right now we have a spelling bee to finish. Meet me after class."

The winner of the spelling bee would determine who would go to the district spelling bee for the entire school system. The young girl missed the second word she was asked to spell. Marvin and the other boy remained standing. Then out of the corner of her eye Mrs. Layman caught a glimpse of a piece of paper the other boy was trying to hide in his hand. She had wondered why he seemed nervous and kept sticking his hands in his pocket. Now she knew. He was cheating.

"Chuck, give me that piece of paper in your hand," Mrs. Layman said, as the class grew exceptionally quiet. They new what was about to happen.

"What, Mrs. Layman? What paper?" Chuck tried to slip the paper in the trash can next to him but the paper missed the can. He was caught. Mrs. Layman picked up the paper to find the list of last week's spelling words written in very small print.

"Chuck, you have just forfeited the spelling bee," Mrs. Layman spoke with authority. "Now, Chuck, you need go to the principal's office and tell him I sent you."

"Marvin, if you can spell the next word correctly, then you will be going to the district spelling bee," Mrs. Layman gave him a big smile. "Spell prophecy."

"P-R-O-P-H-E-C-Y", Marvin spelled.

"That's correct, Marvin. You have won the spelling bee," Mrs. Layman said, as Chuck and the principal, with paddle in hand, appeared at the door. "Class, I have to go right outside the door to witness the principal's paddling Robert. Work on the math homework assignment I gave you this morning."

Sitting at the soda shop over lunch, Marvin and Robert recounted the events of the morning. "Robert, you know, I believe Mom was right when she said, 'honesty is always the best policy.'"

## Questions for Reflection

1. There's an old saying, "Never judge a book by its cover". This means we should not judge people by their looks or outward circumstances. How does this apply to this story?
2. There is another old saying, "You can't pick the family you were born into; but, you can sure choose who your friends are". How was Marvin wise in his choice of friends in the story?
3. Do you think Mrs. Layman was a good teacher? Why or why not?
4. Why do you think Marvin returned the money instead of splitting the money with Chuck?
5. Why is studying and being honest in school important? How did Marvin's honesty and hard work pay off for him?
6. Chuck received a spanking for his dishonesty. This story happened when teachers and principals could paddle students. Have you ever gotten in trouble at school? What happened?

## The following Scriptures are other Bible verses and how they apply to "Honesty Wins a Friend":

| Scripture Reference: | Application: |
| --- | --- |
| Exodus 20:15; Deuteronomy 5:19 | Marvin's honesty |
| Proverbs 18:24 | Marvin's being nice to Robert |
| Proverbs 23:13-14; 29:15 | Chuck's spanking |

# A Child's Prayer

"Daddy, are you going to my play at church next Sunday?" five year old Jennifer asked her father as she rode between him and her mother in the cardinal red Ford mustang. Jennifer and her mother needed him to drive them to choir practice with the family's second car not running.

"Now, Jennifer, you know I don't go to church," her father said. "I visit your grandparents at the nursing home on Sundays."

"I know, Daddy. But, please, just this once. I'm going to be an angel. Don't you want to watch me?"

"Honey, we'll talk about this later," said her father as he pulled the car to a stop on The People's Church parking lot. "Right now you need to go practice."

"Okay, Daddy," Jennifer said hopping out of the car with her long, dark auburn ponytail bobbing in the cold, crisp wind.

"Mommy, why doesn't Daddy want to see my play?" Jennifer, frowning with her thin lips, asked her mother. Mother and daughter walked hand in hand across the church parking lot to the double glass doors of the church.

"Jennifer, Sweetie, it's not that Daddy doesn't want to watch you. He won't go to church. He gets mad when I invite him. We'll talk about this later. Right now you need to put on your big bright smile that you always wear for your friends. Now, where's that smile?"

Jennifer smiled as her dimpled cheeks gave a blushing red over her high cheekbones. Upon entering the building, Jennifer ran from her mother's view down the hall to choir. She arrived first. Her dark chocolate brown eyes sparkled as she smiled at her teachers and other classmates as they arrived.

When Jennifer's teacher, Miss Anna, placed crayons and an angel picture in front of her on the table, Jennifer grabbed an orange crayon and bent her heart-shaped face over the angel. She marked each stroke slowly. *I'll have to take my picture to Daddy,* Jennifer thought. *Maybe then he'll come to church.*

"Would you sing our monthly hymn so you can get your surprise?" Miss Anna asked Jennifer interrupting her thoughts.. "Tonight is the last night, or you won't get the surprise."

"No, Miss Anna." Jennifer shook her head as she continued to color.

"You know the words, Jennifer. Will you sing for me?" said Brian, another teacher helping Miss Anna.

"No." Jennifer continued shaking her head as her ponytail bobbed, revealing the bright red yarn of her name tag against the solid blue collar of the western shirt she wore with blue jeans and black moccasins.

"I want everyone to come here and sit around me in the corner on the floor for the next part of class," said Brian.

Jennifer sat next to Brian's right side. She laid her head on his shoulder as he explained "An eighth note is half of a quarter note."

As Brian talked, Jennifer patted his shoulder thinking, *he is so nice. I wish Daddy would come to church like Brian.*

After Brian's lesson, Miss Michelle, the third teacher in the class, said to Jennifer, "You need to sing our hymn 'I have decided' so you'll get your surprise. Will you sing it for me?"

Again Jennifer shook her head as tears trickled down her pale cheeks. "No."

"Why, Jennifer?" Miss Michelle said. "You're crying. What's wrong?"

"Daddy won't come watch me next Sunday."

"Maybe he'll change his mind," Brian said. "Let's say a prayer right now." Brian grabbed Miss Jennifer's and Miss Michelle's hands pulling them into a circle. "Do you want to pray, Jennifer?"

"Yes, please." Jennifer bowed her head and closed her tear-filled eyes.

"Dear God, I first want to thank You for my teachers and for the fun I've had coloring tonight. God, You know how much I want Daddy at next Sunday's play to watch me perform. Would You please change his mind? He won't listen to me and Mommy.

Maybe Daddy will listen to You. Maybe Grandma and Granddad would feel well enough to come see me also. Would You help them feel better by next Sunday? Please, God. I love You so much. Amen."

The following week each night before going to sleep, Jennifer knelt by her bed. "God, this is Jennifer. Daddy hasn't said he'd come watch me in the church play Sunday. Will You keep after him to change his mind? I want him and my grandparents to come. Please let Grandma and Granddad want to come so Daddy will come. I'll call Grandma Saturday morning at the nursing home while Daddy takes my brother to ball practice. Okay? God. Amen."

"This is Jennifer Knight. May I please speak to my grandmother, Alice Knight?"
"Yes, just a moment please."
"This is Alice Knight."
"Grandma. This is Jenny. How are you and Granddad feeling today?"
"Hi, Jenny. I appreciate your calling. We're feeling better. Are you doing okay?"
"Yes, Grandma. I wanted to invite you and Granddad to my play at church tomorrow. I invited Daddy. He said he had to visit you. But, if you're not there, then he'd have to come to the play to watch me. Will you come, please? You and Granddad haven't been to church for a while. I miss your being there."
"Let me talk to Granddad and your father later. I can't give you a definite answer now. But I hope you know I would like to see you perform. I have to go now. Someone else is waiting to use the telephone. I love you, my little Jenny."
"I love you, Grandma. Bye."

"Jennifer, are you and your mother ready for me to take you to church?" her father asked as he turned off the Sunday Matinee Thriller Movie and walked towards the door to the garage. "I have to go to the nursing home after I take you to church. So please hurry."

*He's not coming to see me in the play*, Jennifer thought, as they traveled the familiar roadway to church. *I guess Grandma forgot to call him and talk to him last night during telephone time at the nursing home.*

At church, Jennifer changed into her white angel costume with her mother's help. "Mommy, I wish Daddy would have come."

"I know, sweetheart. You go out there and do your very best. Remember God is always watching you."

"Okay, Mommy. I love you." Jennifer, smiling, hugged her mother. She ran to take her position on stage behind the curtain.

*I still wish Daddy were here*, Jennifer thought as the curtain rose. Then suddenly in front of her sitting on the front pew were her father, Grandma and Granddad. She also noticed several other residents she knew from the nursing home. "Thank You, God," Jennifer whispered to herself. *Daddy did come after all*, she thought.

After the play Jennifer ran into her father's arms. "Thank you, Daddy! Thank you, Daddy! I didn't think you were coming," she said, as she cried tears of joy to see her father and grandparents at her play.

The next Sunday morning Jennifer's father attended Sunday school and church with his parents, his wife, and both children. At the invitation during the worship service he went forward to accept Christ as his Lord and Savior. Two weeks later he was baptized into The People's Church Fellowship. Jennifer said to her father the day of his baptism, "I'm so happy you'll be going to Heaven too."

"Me too, Jennifer," he said. "It was your and your mother's witness that led me to the Cross."

## Questions for Reflection

1. Why was Jennifer upset with her father? Have you ever been upset with your parents? What happened?
2. Why do you think Jennifer might not have wanted to sing the hymn, "I Have Decided to Follow Jesus"?
3. Why do you think Jennifer's father did not want to come to church at first? What do you think changed his mind?
4. What did Jennifer and her mother do to influence her father to come to church?
5. Who is your favorite character in this story? Why?
6. Why had Jennifer's grandparents not been to church in a while? Is it ever okay for us to stay home from church?
7. How do you think a person gets to Heaven? Do you want to go to Heaven?

## The following Scriptures are other Bible verses and how they apply to "A Child's Prayer":

| Scripture Reference: | Application: |
| --- | --- |
| 1 Peter 3:1-2 | Mrs. Knight's witness before Mr. Knight |
| 1 Peter 2:1-3; 2 Timothy 2:15 | Attending Sunday school |
| Colossians 1:3-6; 1 Peter 5:7 | Jennifer's prayer |

## Building Trust Takes Time

"Jan, don't make any plans with your friends after church Sunday." Eight year old blue-eyed, blonde-headed Jan rode in the front passenger's seat as her mother drove her to school. "Your uncle Bob is having dinner with us."

*Oh, no, not again*, Jan thought as she closed the car door to the country blue Sedan and heard her mother yell, "Hurry, Jan! Get inside before the rain starts!" As Jan walked to her third grade class, she shivered as she remembered Uncle Bob's stay with them the year before after her own father's death. Jennifer's father had been killed the previous year in the line of duty working as a State Trooper. He also served as a deacon at church. After his death, Uncle Bob took advantage of Jennifer and her mother's grief making the excuse that he needed to live with them to take care of the handyman chores around the house. However, Uncle Bob had other ulterior motives.

"Where's the money?!" her mother yelled at Uncle Bob. "Three hundred dollars is missing from my kitty."

"Don't ask me," Uncle Bob said. "I don't know what happened to your money. Maybe you misplaced the bills."

"No, I have a notebook where I record every cent that is added to, or taken away from my kitty." Jan ran to her bedroom. She heard her mother and Uncle Bob's voices as she sat shivering in the bedroom closet.

"Maybe Jan took the money," Uncle Bob said. *Now he's blaming me*, Jan thought. *I wish he hadn't come here to live.*

"Don't blame Jan!" her mother yelled. "I know her better than that. Besides, she can't reach the shelf where I keep the kitty. You took my money. Now don't lie to me."

"Why would I lie?"

"Because of the drinking," her mother said. "You stole the money to buy alcohol."

"What if I did?" Uncle Bob said. "You're not hurting for cash."

"That isn't the point!" her mother screamed. "The point is you need help. If I have anymore trouble from you, I'll kick you out. What will you do then?"

"Now, Beatrice," Uncle Bob said. "Just calm down. You don't mean that."

"Yes, I do," Beatrice said. "Try me, and you'll see I'm serious."

Later that evening Jan sat at the dinner table to do her homework. Uncle Bob walked into the kitchen. "Jan, do you have a couple of dollars you'd loan your uncle?"

"No, I don't." Jan looked up from her work at her uncle. "I'm saving my allowance to go on a trip with my Sunday school class. You know you should go to Sunday school and church."

"I'll pay you back," Uncle Bob said glaring at Jan. "Now, give me your money."

"No!" Jan turned her gaze to the arithmetic assignment on the table.

"Yes, you will." Uncle Bob grabbed Jan's arm pulling her from her chair. "Now, where's your money?"

"I'm not telling," Jan said as she freed herself from her uncle's grasp.

"Yes, you will." Uncle Bob jerked her from her seat again.

"No, she won't," Beatrice interrupted. "Now get out of here. I warned you."

*Why does Mom want Uncle Bob to come visit now?* Jan thought. *Without him around this past year, our life has been peaceful. Besides, Uncle Bob scares me. I'll have to talk to Mom about this after school this evening.*

"Mom, why is Uncle Bob coming here Sunday?" Jan and Beatrice sat at the dinner table eating tacos and refried beans. "I don't want to be here to see Uncle Bob. He scares me."

"He scares you. Why, Jan? Bob loves you."

"Don't you remember last year when he stayed here? He scared me then."

"I know, Jan. But your uncle wasn't himself then. His behavior was from his drinking. He's not drinking now. He's changed. Please give him a chance. Okay?"

"Okay, I'll try." Jan reached for her glass of lemonade as she swallowed her last bite of Taco. The next Sunday Jan sat quietly next to her mother's right side as worship service was about to begin. Suddenly, she felt someone sliding into the seat on her right nudge her shoulder. Jan looked to the right.

"Hi, Jan." Uncle Bob reached his arm around Jan to pat Beatrice on the shoulder.

"Hi, Bob," Beatrice said. "I'm so glad you came today. Jan say 'hello' to Bob."

"Hi, Uncle Bob," Jan said, as the minister walked to the pulpit to welcome the guests. *Uncle Bob surprised me by coming to church this morning*, Jan thought. She slid closer to her mother on the pew. *He frightens me.*

After worship service Uncle Bob turned to face her. "You sang beautifully in church this morning, Jan," he said. "How has my favorite niece been doing?"

"Okay, I guess," Jan said.

"Would you like to ride with me to your house for dinner? We haven't talked recently."

"No, I'm going with Mom." Jan reached for her mother's hand as her uncle tried to hug her.

"Jan, that was rude of you to not let Bob hug you after church," her mother said as they traveled home. "Aren't you glad he came to church today?"

"I guess so. But he scares me because I remember what happened the last time he was at our house."

"I know, Jan," her mother said, pulling into the driveway. "You'll have to forgive Bob. I know forgetting can be hard."

"The turkey tastes great, and is so tender, Mom." Jan, her mother and uncle sat at the dinner table. *You can't beat Mom's cooking*, Jan thought, *but Uncle Bob's being here makes me nervous.*

"What's wrong, Jan?" her uncle said. "You seem so fidgety. You didn't used to be so restless."

"I don't want to talk about it."

"Why, Jan? I'm your uncle. You can talk to me about anything. What's wrong?"

"I'm afraid of you."

". . . Afraid of me?" Her uncle laid down his fork as he turned his full attention to her. "Why, Jan? I wouldn't do anything to hurt you."

"She remembers what happened last year," Beatrice interrupted. "You may not remember. You scared her whenever you were drunk."

"I'm sorry, Jan." Her uncle patted her shoulder. "After your mother kicked me out to live on the streets last year, I realized the error of my ways. I admitted myself to a hospital. I've quit drinking. I'm working now. I also have an apartment. Will you try to forgive me?"

"I'll try. Forgetting may take me a while though."

"I know, Jan," her uncle said as he picked up his fork. "I have to be patient also. You won't trust me overnight. That will take time."

Months went by with Uncle Bob coming to church every Sunday and then coming over to eat Sunday dinner with Jan and her mother. Jan kept her distance for a while. Then Uncle Bob started dating Jan's Sunday school teacher Ms. Kay.

"Ms. Kay, why do you date my uncle?" Jan asked her teacher one Sunday morning. "He scares me."

"Why, Jan, Bob is a fine man. He and I were friends in high school. He wanted to date me before now but I refused because I didn't want to be unequally yoked with a non believer. Your uncle is a changed man now."

"But, Ms. Kay, he was mean to mean a couple of years ago when he lived with mom and me," Jan shared the rest of her story, closing with, "He hurt me, Ms. Kay."

"Jan, honey, we've all done things we aren't proud of. You have to forgive people, as Christ forgives us. Trust me, Jan, Bob won't hurt you anymore." Soon Bob and Ms. Kay began asking

Jan to go to the park, to movies and on other dates as "our little chaperone", they called her.

With the end of the school year approaching, the Father/Daughter Banquet was over the horizon. One Sunday morning Jan said to Ms. Kay after Sunday school, "I know Uncle Bob is your boyfriend, Ms. Kay. I wanted to ask you, is it okay if he takes me on a date to the Father/Daughter Banquet at school?" Ms. Kay chuckled.

"Yes, of course, that's okay, Jan," Ms. Kay said smiling as she saw Bob walking down the hall to meet her for church. "I think that can be arranged."

"Bob, this young lady would like you to take her to the Father/Daughter Banquet at school. She asked me for my permission. Do you want to be her date?"

"I'd be honored to be her date," Bob smiled at his niece. "I'm just grateful she has forgiven and trusts me now." Three weeks later Jan had her first date with Uncle Bob taking her to the Father/Daughter Banquet.

## Questions for Reflection

1. How do you think Jan felt after her father's death? What about Jan's mother? How would she have felt? Have you ever had anyone close to you die?
2. Why did Jan's mother kick Uncle Bob out of the house?
3. Why was Jan afraid of Uncle Bob?
4. Why did Jan's mother welcome Uncle Bob back into the home later?
5. Why did Ms. Kay not want to get in a serious relationship with Bob at first?
6. Why do you think Jan gave her uncle a second chance?
7. What is your favorite part of the story? Why?

## The following Scriptures are other Bible verses and how they apply to "Building Trust Takes Time":

| Scripture Reference: | Application: |
|---|---|
| Ephesians 5:18; Proverbs 29:30-35; Galatians 5:19-21 | Uncle Bob's drinking |
| 2 Corinthians 6:14-15 | Ms. Kay not dating Bob at first |
| Ephesians 4:32 | Jan and her mother forgiving Bob |

# Christian Takes Time to Touch a Life

"Christian, do you want to go to the playoffs next Friday night?" 10 year old Christian's father said as he drove Christian to football practice. "I can get tickets for us."

"Sure, Dad," Christian said as his father pulled the red Mercedes on the parking lot of his team's playing field. "You couldn't pay me to miss a chance to attend the playoffs."

"I'll pick you up after practice," his father said. Christian ran towards his coach on the practice field.

"Coach, Dad is taking me to the playoffs next Friday. Isn't that great?"

"Yes, that's thoughtful of your father," Coach Travis said. "I think you'll learn a lot watching the pros. But right now you need to get out there with your teammates."

"Okay, Coach." Christian ran towards his teammates in a huddle.

"Hey, guys! Guess what?" Christian yelled. "Dad is taking me to the playoffs next Friday. Isn't that great?"

"That's cool!", "That's great!" and "You're lucky!" came from the huddle. Christian joined the circle.

"I can't wait! I'm excited! You won't be able to stand being around me this next week."

"That's okay, Christian," Allen, his locker partner, said. "Make sure you share every detail with us afterwards."

"No problem." Christian grinned.

"Christian, I bought our tickets today for the playoffs next Friday," Christian's father said as they waited for Christian's mother to bring them a piece of blueberry cobbler.

"Gee, thanks, Dad," Christian said. "Coach says I should learn a lot from watching the professionals."

"Yes, I think the experience will be good for you."

"Mom, will you be going with us?" Christian asked his mother as she sat a piece of cobbler with vanilla ice cream in front of him.

"No, Christian," his mother said. "Next weekend is the spiritual enrichment conference for women at church. My planning to attend the conference is one reason your father decided to take you to the playoffs. He said he'd be bored with my being gone all weekend."

"Okay, Mom. We'll miss you."

"Thanks, Christian. I'm sure you won't miss me too much with the excitement at the playoffs."

Between school, football practice, band and youth activities at church, Christian thought little about the upcoming playoffs the next week until Friday morning as his father drove him to school. "Dad, are we still going to the playoffs this evening?"

"You better believe we're going. Your mother leaves this afternoon for the women's conference. Do you want to go somewhere for pizza after the game?"

"That sounds fine with me," Christian said as he opened the car door to the Mercedes. "I'll see you later at home." Christian ran towards the school building. *I can't wait until this school day is over,* he thought. *This should be the best weekend Dad and I have had since we went fishing last summer.*

"Christian, is your father still planning to take you to the playoffs this evening?" Allen said. The two boys stood by their locker.

"Yes, we're going. Then we're going somewhere for pizza. I wish you could join us."

"Me too," Allen said as he opened the locker. "Your plans sound fun."

*I'm hyper about tonight's game,* Christian thought as he sat in history class. *I can't concentrate on what Ms. Jiles is saying.* Across the room he noticed the new boy who had moved three houses down the street from his family's home. *I'll have to talk to him after class.*

# Fiction for the Children

"Christian, are you paying attention?" Ms. Jiles interrupted his thoughts. "I asked everyone to pull out a sheet of paper and pencil for a pop quiz."

"Oh, I'm sorry, Ms. Jiles," Christian said. He reached into his notebook for a clean sheet of paper. Christian's face flushed. *I better get my mind on history*, he thought.

After class Christian approached the new boy across the room. "Hi, I'm Christian. I noticed you moved down the street from my family."

"Oh, hi. I'm Greg. I've seen you around. How long have you lived there?"

"My family moved to town about three years ago from Florida," Christian said. "Where's your hometown?"

"We moved from Dallas, Texas," Greg said as he turned to exit the classroom. "I enjoyed meeting you. However, right now I have to hurry home. My grandparents are coming to visit us. I haven't seen them in several years."

"I understand, Greg. I have a big evening planned myself. My father is taking me to the playoffs. We'll get together later. Have fun with your grandparents."

*Dad won't be home for 45 minutes*, Christian thought as he took his time walking home. About three blocks from home Christian heard sirens approaching from behind him. Ahead of Christian, he could see a crowd gathering at the end of his block. *I wonder what is happening*, Christian thought. He began running. He watched the fire truck slow to a stop at the next corner as he neared the scene. Greg laid in the middle of the crowd on the road.

"What happened?" Christian yelled as he approached the firefighters checking the injuries to Greg's body. *He must be hurt badly*, Christian thought.

"Does anyone know this boy? Who is he?" a firefighter asked as he turned from facing Greg to the onlookers. No one answered.

"His name is Greg," Christian said. "He lives a few houses down the street. Can I help? I'll run to get his family."

"Thanks a lot, Son," the firefighter said. "Please hurry. Greg is unconscious."

"Okay, sir." Christian ran his fastest as he approached Greg's house. *Oh, no, the driveway is empty*, Christian thought. *I hope someone is home.*

Christian rang the doorbell with one hand. He banged on the door with his other fist. No answer.

Christian returned to the accident scene. "No one is home," Christian said.

"Mom, Dad, I want my parents," Greg cried in a weak voice. Christian stepped to Greg's side.

"Greg, this is Christian from school who lives down the street from you. Remember? No one is at your house. Where are your parents?"

"I don't know," Greg said faintly. "Please don't leave me."

"Don't worry. I won't." Out of the corner of his eye, Christian noticed his father's car approaching in the distance. *Good, at least, my dad will be here*, Christian thought. *He'll know what to do.*

"Dad, this is Greg," Christian said as his father walked to his side. "Remember the new boy in my class from down the street. We have to help him. None of his family is home."

"How's the boy?" Christian's father directed his question to the paramedic inserting an IV needle in Greg's arm.

"He needs to be taken to the hospital by ambulance," the paramedic answered. "He might have a concussion."

"Christian, what do you want to do?" Christian's father knelt by Greg. "If we don't leave now, we'll miss the playoffs. You make the choice."

"Dad, what if this were me lying there?" Christian said. "Of course, we'll stay with Greg---that's what any Christian would do."

As soon as the paramedics had Greg stable, Christian's father, an assistant pastor at the local church, asked the paramedics whether he could pray with Greg. "Go ahead," the senior paramedic said.

"Heavenly Father, I come to You now in the name of Your Son Jesus Christ asking that You touch the body of Greg right now. May he not have any serious injuries? Remove all fear from Greg, and help him to find comfort in Your presence here. Give the paramedics and doctors wisdom. Comfort and guide Greg's family as they deal with this situation. Again, we ask for Your healing touch upon Greg's body, mind, and soul. Amen."

"Thank you, Sir. That was a fine prayer", an older man who had appeared in the crowd during the prayer said. "That's my grandson. Will he be okay? What happened?

"Apparently, it was a hit and run. No one saw the accident," a police officer said. "Where are his parents?"

"There is his father coming now." The older man pointed to a middle aged man running down the street about half a block away. "I called him on my cell phone when I realized Greg was the one hurt."

"How's my boy? Is he okay?" Greg's father said as he caught his breath.

"Dad, I'm alright! I just have a headache!" Greg had heard his father's voice in the crowd.

"He might have a concussion," the senior paramedic said. "We recommend we take him to the hospital in the ambulance to get checked out."

"Do whatever they tell you to do, Son," Greg's father said.

"Okay, Dad," Greg smiled faintly. "First, I want to thank Christian and his father for staying with me until you and Gramps got here. Thank you, Christian! If I remember correctly, you and your dad were going to the playoffs. I don't want you missing the game because of me. Now go have fun at the game. I'll see you at school Monday."

"We'll only be about 15 minutes late if we hurry," Christian's father said.

"Okay, Dad, let's go," Christian headed for the car. "Greg, I'll check on you later."

Christian and his father made the playoffs after all. They even went out for pizza as they had planned. The next morning Christian and his father went to visit Greg who was home recuperating with a broken ankle and a mild concussion. Greg and Christian remained friends for a lifetime.

## Questions for Reflection

1. Why was Christian not paying attention in his history class? Have you ever gotten in trouble for not paying attention? What happened?
2. Why did Christian say he and his father would not go to the playoffs after the accident? How do you think this made Greg feel?
3. Have you ever made plans for something special like Christian did and had to change those plans at the last minute? What were your plans? How were the plans changed?
4. What do you think about the person who hit and left Greg alone? What should he/she have done?
5. How did Christian and his family reflect Christ in their lives?
6. Who was your favorite character in the story? Why?
7. What should you do if you ever come upon an accident like Christian did?

## The following Scriptures are other Bible verses and how they apply to "Christian Takes Time to Touch a Life:

| Scripture Reference: | Application: |
| --- | --- |
| 1 Peter 5:2-4 | Christian's father's good example as a pastor |
| James 5:14-15 | Christian's father's praying for Greg |
| Luke 10:25-37 (Parable of the Good Samaritan) | Christian's stopping to help Greg |

# Patience's Prayers Prevent Peril

"Patience, please don't tell anyone what I told you," Amber, Patience's new friend, said. "Can you come over so we can talk more?" The two 12 year olds walked home from school. They had met three months earlier after Amber and her family moved to the white A-frame house across the street from Patience. Patience lived in a two-story red brick house with her parents.

"I don't know," Patience said. "I'll have to ask my parents. I'll call you."

"Mom, Amber asked if I could come over now." Patience laid her school books on the coffee table.

"Are her parents home?" Patience's mother said as she sat on the emerald green couch hemming a pair of blue jeans. "I don't want you over there without an adult to supervise."

"I don't know, Mom. I told Amber I'd call her. I'll ask whenever I call."

"Okay, Patience. Let me know what she says."

Patience retrieved her homework on the coffee table to finish in her bedroom. Upstairs in her bedroom Patience looked out the window to see the A-Frame across the street. *All the cars are gone*, Patience thought. *I don't think Amber's parents are home. I'll call to double-check.*

"Hello, this is Amber."

"Amber, this is Patience. Are your parents home? Mom said I can't come over without an adult there to supervise."

"No, I'm the only one home. Even if Mom and Dad were here, they wouldn't do much supervising. They keep to themselves. Can you come over now?"

"No, I better wait. I'll call back after I finish my homework. Maybe Mom will let you eat dinner with us. Are you hungry?"

"No, but I'll be hungry by dinner time. Give me a call in a while."

"Okay, Amber. I need to work on my spelling lesson now. Bye."

Patience sat at her desk unscrambling the letters to make words in her spelling assignment. *Maybe Amber will confide in Mom and Dad*, she thought. *I hope Mom lets Amber eat dinner with us. I'll go ask now.*

"Mom, the rest of Amber's family is gone. Can Amber eat dinner with us?"

"Sure, I've got lasagna baking in the oven. Garden salad is in the refrigerator. And I'm fixing garlic bread. Setting an extra plate isn't any problem."

"Thanks, Mom." Patience ran to her room to call Amber. *I wonder where Amber's mother is now*, she thought as she noticed the driveway across the street empty. *Mom wouldn't leave me at home alone like Amber's parents have left her.*

"Amber, I'm so glad you could have dinner with us." Patience's mother passed the bread basket around the table. "Do you like garlic bread, Amber?"

"Yes, I do. Mom doesn't cook much though. This is a treat for me."

"Well, I hope you enjoy my cooking," Patience's mother said as she cut into the steaming lasagna. "Pass me your plate, Amber."

"Thank you, Mrs. Douglas." Amber passed her plate to Patience's mother. "The lasagna smells great."

"Mom's lasagna is better than what they serve at school," Patience said.

"Anything is better than what they serve at school," Amber said. Everyone laughed.

"Amber, you said your mother doesn't cook much," Patience's father said. "Does she work outside of the home?"

"No, . . . she doesn't like cooking." Amber's face flushed as she fidgeted in her chair.

"Is something wrong?" Patience's mother said. "Where are your parents now?"

"I don't know. They weren't at home."

"We don't leave Patience here alone." Patience's father reached for his iced tea. "Anything could happen. You can't trust people like you could years ago."

"Sometimes you can't trust your family," Amber mumbled as she sipped her tea.

"What do you mean by that?" Patience's mother said frowning.

"Oh, nothing . . . it's nothing," Amber said with tear-filled eyes. "May I have another slice of garlic bread?"

"Sure, there's plenty," Patience said as she handed the basket to Amber. *I wish Amber would tell mom and dad*, she thought. *Someone might get hurt over there.*

"Amber, you could have told Mom and Dad at dinner," Patience said as the two girls worked a puzzle on the playroom floor. "I'm afraid someone might get hurt at your house."

"Everything will get better. Please don't tell anyone. You promised. Be patient with me. Okay?"

"Okay." Patience connected the last side piece to the puzzle. *I don't know how long I can keep her secret*, she thought. *I'll have to pray about this situation.*

Patience knelt by her bed for her prayer time. "Dear God, thank You for the fun time I had with Amber this evening. I want to pray for her and her family now. Please protect Amber. Please don't let Amber's father hit her, her mother or the baby anymore. Make him get help. I like Amber, God. Having a friend close across the street is nice, since I don't have a brother or sister to keep me company. I'd tell Mom and Dad myself; but, I promised Amber I wouldn't tell anyone. Please help them. Amen."

"Patience, would you like to invite Amber to spend the night Friday night?", her mother asked as Patience ate her oatmeal and toast the next morning. "From Amber's remarks yesterday evening at dinner, she seems lonely. I thought you two might enjoy a slumber party."

"Really, that sounds great! Thanks, Mom. I'll ask Amber at school."

"Amber, would you want to spend the night at my house tomorrow night? Mom said we could have a slumber party."

"Sure, I haven't been to a sleep over in a long time," Amber said as she unwrapped a peanut butter sandwich for lunch. "I hope you didn't tell your parents."

"No, I haven't told anyone," Patience said. She opened the can of fruit cocktail her mother packed for her lunch. "We'll talk more about that tomorrow night."

"We've almost finished the puzzle," Amber said to Patience as they sat on the playroom floor eating popcorn. "What can we do next?"

"Girls, I need to talk to you." Patience's mother entered the room. "I want to know what is going on at Amber's house?"

"You told, Patience." Tears rolled down Amber's cheeks as she spoke.. "How could you? I thought you were my friend."

"No, Amber. Patience didn't tell anyone." Patience's mother patted Amber on the shoulder. "She is your friend. I overheard her praying the other night. Please don't be mad at Patience."

"Why didn't you tell me what you heard, Mom?"

"I wanted to talk to both of you together. Amber, I don't want to see you hurt." Patience's mother hugged Amber. "Also as a law-abiding citizen, I have to try to get help for your family. Will you work with me so you won't be in danger anymore?"

"Sure, Mrs. Douglas." Amber sobbed in her arms. Patience patted her friend's shoulder.

## Questions for Reflection

1. Why did Patience's mother not allow her to go to Amber's house without adult supervision?
2. Patience prayed for her friend Amber. Do you pray for your friends? Why or why not?
3. How did Patience reflect Christ in her life?
4. Why did Patience not tell her mother that Amber's parents were mean to the children?
5. When Patience's mother overheard her daughter's prayer, why did she not talk to Patience right then about what she heard?
6. What should you do if you learn that a parent or other adult is being mean to a child?
7. Who was your favorite character in the story? Why?

---

## The following Scriptures are other Bible verses and how they apply to "Patience's Prayers Prevent Peril":

| Scripture Reference: | Application: |
| --- | --- |
| Hebrews 4:16 | Patience praying for Amber |
| Genesis 37:12-36 | Biblical example of child abuse |
| Mark 4:22; Luke 12:2-3 | Child abuse being revealed |

## Lying Lips Lose

"Karen, I want you to clean your bedroom today," her mother said as she woke the eight year old red head. "I won't have your friends here next weekend for your birthday party with your room in a mess."

"Do I have to clean my room today?" Karen said yawning. "Patty wanted me to come over today."

"You may go to Patty's after you clean your room. Put your old toys in a box. Put the boxes in the garage. Then your father will take them to church for charity."

"Okay, Mom." Karen sat up in bed. "Are you helping me?"

"No, I have to do laundry and straighten up the family room." Her mother turned towards the door. "You're big enough to pick up after yourself."

Karen changed from her hot pink nightshirt into a pair of blue jeans, a navy T-shirt and tennis shoes. The telephone rang.

"Karen, Patty is on the telephone!" her mother yelled from the downstairs den. "You may use the phone in my bedroom! Remember what I said!"

"Okay, Mom!" Karen ran to her parents' bedroom. She picked up the receiver.

"Patty, this is Karen. Mom said I can come over after I clean my room."

"How long will that take? Mom said you could go with us to the zoo today. She'll pay your way."

"What time did you want me to be ready to leave?"

"About 10 o'clock. It's eight thirty now."

"Don't worry. I'll be ready." Karen quickly hung up the receiver. She dashed to her room to finish her chore. *I'll have to hurry*, she thought.

Karen made her bed. Then she took her dirty clothes to the laundry room.

"Mom, I need some empty boxes." Karen handed her mother the dirty clothes. "Where are they? I need to hurry. After I clean my room, Patty's mom said she'd take us to the zoo."

"You may go to the zoo as long as your room is cleaned first. Look in the garage next to the work bench for boxes."

"I can't find any boxes," Karen grumbled to herself. *Dad must have thrown them away*, she thought. *Patty and her mother will be here soon. I'll put my old toys in the closet or under the bed where no one can see them.*

As she stuffed the last puzzle under her bed Karen heard a car pull into the driveway. *That must be Patty and her mother*, she thought. Karen grabbed her light blue wind breaker hanging in the closet.

"Is that Patty?" her mother shouted from downstairs. "Have you finished your chores like I told you?"

"Yes, Mom! I'm leaving!" Karen yelled as she pulled the front door behind her.

"Hi, Patty! Hi, Mrs. Johnson! Thanks for inviting me to go with you."

"You're welcome, Karen," Mrs. Johnson said as she backed the tan Ford station wagon out of the driveway. "Consider the invitation an early birthday present."

"Okay, thanks. Are you letting Patty come to my party Saturday?"

"Of course. I know both of you are best friends. I wouldn't want her to miss your birthday celebration."

"Karen, is your room straight?" her mother said. "Your friends will be here soon for your party."

"Yes, Mom." Karen threw her beach bag onto the top shelf of her closet. The front doorbell rang. Karen ran to answer the living room door.

"Hi, Patty! Hi, Sandra!" The girls hugged.

"Happy birthday, Karen!" Patty and Sandra said simultaneously. "Are Bonnie and Helen here yet?"

"No, you two are the first to arrive," Karen said as she noticed Bonnie's mother's green Nova turning the corner. "Oh, here comes Bonnie and Helen now."

"I'm glad we're not the only ones late," Patty said. "We decided at the last minute to go swimming at the "Y" after your party. I had to get my swimming gear together."

"That sounds fun. If there's room in the car, maybe Mom will let me go with you."

"Sure, Karen," Patty said as she handed Karen her present. "The more the merrier. Dad will pick us up in the van in a couple of hours."

"Great! I'll ask Mom." Karen walked into the dining room where her mother poured fruit punch for the five girls. Patty, Sandra, Bonnie and Helen followed Karen.

"Mom, after my party, may I go to the "Y" with Patty and Sandra?"

"Patty, how long did you plan to be gone?" Karen's mother paused pouring the girls' drinks. "Karen's grandparents planned to stop by this evening to give her a present."

"Oh, we'll be gone a couple of hours." Patty accepted the punch handed to her by Karen's mother. "We'll have her home by six o'clock this evening."

"Let me call her grandparents to ask what time they expect to get here." Karen's mother turned to exit the room. "You girls have fun. I'll be in the laundry room. Let me know if you need anything."

The five girls sat around the table where Karen's mother had set five plates of birthday cake and ice cream. A bowl of potato chips, dip, party hats, balloons and the remaining cake filled the middle of the table.

"I love this chocolate birthday cake, Karen!" Patty said as she reached for a second piece. "My mom always bakes a white cake for my birthday."

"Mom knows chocolate is my favorite flavor."

"You're lucky, Karen!" The other girls chimed simultaneously. "Your mother is special."

"Karen, your grandparents won't be here until about seven o'clock this evening," her mother said entering the dining room door. "I guess you may go to the "Y". Do you girls need anything?"

"No, thank you, Mrs. Fields," Patty said as she looked at her Minnie Mouse wrist watch. "Dad will be here any minute to pick us up."

"That must be your father now," Karen said. "I thought I heard a van pull into the driveway. Patty, will you get my beach bag out of my closet? I'll see Bonnie and Helen to the door."

"Bye, Bonnie. Bye, Helen. Thanks for coming to my party." As Karen shut the front door, a crash sounded from upstairs. *Oh, no*, Karen thought, *what's happened.*

"Karen, what was that noise?" her mother said running upstairs.

"I hit my head, Mrs. Fields. Karen asked me to get her beach bag out of the closet. When I reached for the handle, everything fell. I'm sorry."

"You're not to blame, Patty." Mrs. Fields entered the bedroom. "Karen, look at this mess. Come here."

"What happened, Mom?" Karen walked from the stairs to her bedroom's doorway.

"Patty got hit in the head with your toys falling out of the closet---the toys I asked you to put in boxes and take to the garage. I know today is your birthday; but, you just lost your privilege to go swimming."

"What! Why, Mom?!" Karen's eyes filled with tears.

"You lied, Karen. Thus, you lose."

## Questions for Reflection

1. Why did Karen's mom want her to clean her room? Do you have chores that you do?
2. How did Karen disobey her mother?
3. Karen assumed that because Patty's mother said she could go to the zoo with them that her mother would approve? Should you tell your parents what you are going to do or ask permission?
4. Why was Patty late for Karen's birthday party? How did this make Karen feel? Have you ever been late for a party or something?
5. How do you think Bonnie and Helen felt when they weren't invited to go swimming?
6. Do you think Karen's mother was right to not let Karen go swimming? Why or Why not?
7. What was your favorite part of the story? Why?

## The following Scriptures are other Bible verses and how they apply to "Lying Lips Lose":

| Scripture Reference: | Application: |
| --- | --- |
| Proverbs 12:22; 19:5 | Karen's lying |
| Proverbs 13:24; 22:15 | Karen's mother's parenting |
| Ephesians 6:1-2 | Karen's disobedience |

> "Giving thanks always for all things to God the Father in the name of our Lord Jesus Christ."
>
> **Ephesians 5:20**

## Attitudes of Gratitude

"Billy, what'll we do for Thanksgiving dinner this year?" Donna overheard eight year old Frankie ask her 11 year old brother. The two orphans sat on the church pew behind Donna.

"I don't know," Billy said. "Since Grandma and Grandpa died, we won't have anywhere special to go this Thanksgiving."

*I feel sorry for Billy and Frankie living at the children's home*, Donna thought. *I wish I could help them.*

After worship service Donna turned to greet the children sitting behind her. "Hi, Billy. Hi, Frankie. How's school going?"

"Frankie makes straight A's in spite of her grief from loosing our grandparents this past year," Billy said. "I'm proud of her. However, I'm struggling with the new math being taught now."

"Good girl!" Donna hugged Frankie. "I'm proud of you also. Keep up the hard work."

"Thank you," Frankie said smiling.

"Do you have a tutor to help you with your math, Billy?"

"No, I'm hoping I do better soon." Billy picked up his and Frankie's Bibles laying on the pew.

"Let me know if you don't," Donna said. "My older brother tutors at the high school. He's a whiz at math. I think he'd be happy to work with you. If he can't, then I'll try to assist you."

"Gee, that would be helpful. Thanks, Donna." Billy turned to walk away with Frankie by his side.

"Jerrod, remember the orphans Billy and Frankie Smith from the children's home," Donna said to her 17 year old brother over a piece of fried chicken during the family's Sunday afternoon meal. "They were at church today. Billy has been having trouble with math. If he keeps having trouble, can you tutor him?"

"Probably not. I'm already working with other students who live at the children's home." Jerrod reached for a piece of

Fiction for the Children 45

cornbread. "You're pretty good at math. If you want, I'd be happy to let you ride with me to the children's home when I go there to work with the other children. You can help Billy."
"That's kind of you, Jerrod. I didn't know you volunteered at the children's home. When did you start doing that?"
"At the beginning of the school year. A social worker for the children's home called the high school. She asked for volunteer tutors to assist them in helping the slower children having problems in school. I'm humbled by the gratitude the children show me. They're eager to learn."
"I know Billy always worked hard at school. I think his parents' fatal accident three years ago, and then his grandparents' deaths this past year set him back. I hope I can help him."

"Billy, is math getting any easier for you?" Billy and Frankie sat on the pew in front of Donna the next Sunday.
"Not really." Billy frowned.
"I talked to my brother. He's already tutoring some students where you live. He said I could ride with him whenever he drives to help them. I'll help you."
"Thanks, Donna." Billy smiled as he put his arm on the seat behind Frankie.
"Jerrod goes to the children's home every Tuesday and Thursday. I'll see you this Tuesday evening about seven o'clock." Donna turned her attention to the soloist approaching the pulpit.

"Hi, Donna." Billy lead Donna and her brother to the dining room doubling as a study area for the residents of the children's home.
"Billy, this is my brother Jerrod."
"Hi, Jerrod. I want to thank you for bringing Donna here to help me with my math homework."
"No problem. Donna talks a lot about you and your sister. She likes both of you." Jerrod walked to the far end of the table where another child waited to be tutored.
"Now let's get to work on your math, Billy." Donna and Billy seated themselves at the table. "What's your homework for today?"

"Look here. We're supposed to do exercises one, three and four on this page." Within the hour, Billy completed his assignment with Donna's coaching.

"Is that all, Billy?"

"Yes, thanks, Donna." Billy closed his math book. "You make math sound simpler than when my teacher explains how to work the problems."

"Good, I'm glad I could help. Rob always works with his student until 8:30 p.m. We've another half an hour to chat."

"Okay. How long have you been going to First Baptist Church?"

"We've always gone there. I knew your grandparents. Mom said they were charter members at church."

"Yes, I knew that." Billy's eyes filled with tears.

"Oh, I'm sorry, Billy." Donna patted his shoulder. "I shouldn't have mentioned your grandparents."

"That's okay, Donna." Billy wiped a tear from his cheek. "With the holidays approaching, I think about our mom, our dad and our grandparents anyway. Frankie and I have no other family."

"Speaking of holidays, I heard Frankie say you didn't have anywhere to spend Thanksgiving. Would you like for me to ask Mom if the two of you can join us that day? Don't mention it to Frankie until I make sure Mom and Dad say okay. I'm certain your spending Thanksgiving with us won't be a problem. Just in case though, I don't want to disappoint Frankie."

"Mom, would you care to set a couple of extra plates this Thanksgiving?" Donna asked her mother, Ada Fields, at breakfast the next morning. "Billy and Frankie don't have any family to spend the holiday with since their grandparents died. May they spend Thanksgiving Day with us?"

"Of course, they may spend Thanksgiving here." Mrs. Fields replied smiling.

"Thanks, Mom." Donna swallowed her last bite of bacon. "I'll ask them Sunday. Thanksgiving is next Thursday."

"Frankie! Billy! Wait a minute!" Donna pushed her way to the pew where the orphans sat four rows behind her in church. "I want to ask you both something." Donna winked at Billy.

"What do you want to ask us?" Frankie said as she hugged Donna.

"Would you like to eat Thanksgiving dinner with my family?" Donna patted Frankie's back as they hugged. "Mom said you can spend the whole day with us. She likes you."

"Billy! Billy! See." Frankie's eyes filled with tears as she smiled. "We'll get to be with a real family this Thanksgiving. That was my prayer this morning."

Happy Thanksgiving, Frankie & Billy!

## Questions for Reflection

1. Why did Donna feel sorry for Frankie and Billy?
2. Billy needed help with his math homework. What did he do to get help with his lessons? Do you ever need help with your lessons? What do you do when you need help?
3. Why did Jerrod volunteer at the children's home? Have you ever helped someone as a volunteer?
4. How did Donna and her family reflect Christ in their lives?
5. What was Frankie's prayer? How was that prayer answered?
6. Who was your favorite character in the story? Why?
7. How does your family spend Thanksgiving? Is there a special Thanksgiving that you remember?

## The following Scriptures are other Bible verses and how they apply to "Attitudes of Gratitude":

| Scripture Reference: | Application: |
| --- | --- |
| 1 Thessalonians 5:18; Philippians 4:6; Psalm 50:14; 107:1; Matthew 6:25-34 | Thanksgiving |
| Psalm 10:14; 68:5 | God looking out for the orphans |
| James 1:27; Exodus 22:22; I John 3:17 | People helping the orphans |

## How do you count your blessings?

- Food
- Clothing
- Shelter
- Transportation
- Family
- Friends
- Church
- School
- Work
- Play
- Health

Can you name others?

## A Forever Family

Thanksgiving had arrived. The orphans Billy and Frankie sat in the back seat of the car as Mr. Fields drove them to the Fields' home where the children would be spending the day. The children, especially Frankie, looked forward to a day away from the children's home.

"Mr. Fields, are we there yet?" Frankie asked. "I can't wait to see everybody!"

"Not yet, Frankie," Mr. Fields replied as he turned the next corner. "This is our street. We're just a few houses down."

"I'm excited, too!" Billy said. "May we watch the parade and then the ballgame today?"

"I see no reason why not," Mr. Fields said as he turned the car into the driveway.

Inside the house was warm and cozy with Mrs. Fields cooking in the kitchen while Donna and Jerrod sat at the kitchen table eating breakfast. "They're here, Mom." Jerrod said. "I hear the car doors shutting."

Mr. Fields was as excited as Billy and Frankie to have them over. "Make your selves at home," he said as he shuffled the children through the front door. *They are going to be surprised*, he thought to himself smiling. "Are you two hungry? Donna and Jerrod were getting ready to eat breakfast when I left to pick up the two of you."

"Frankie was too excited this morning to eat breakfast, and I can always make room for your wife's cooking," Billy said as Mrs. Fields and the children entered the front room to greet Billy and Frankie.

"That was sweet of you to say, Billy" Mrs. Fields said as she ushered everyone into the kitchen. "Let's say grace with everyone here now, and then we'll eat. After that, I need to get the turkey and other trimmings started for dinner."

After breakfast Mr. Fields and the children retreated to the living room to watch the day's festivities on the big screen television. A few minutes into the parade, a knock came from the door.

"That must be your grandparents, Jerrod," Mr. Fields said. "Would you answer the door?"

"Sure, Dad", Jerrod said as he got up to unlock the door. "You didn't tell us they were coming too."

"We wanted to surprise you children," Mr. Fields replied.

Jerrod was further surprised when he opened the door to see both sets of his grandparents waiting at the door. "Wow, I can't believe it! The whole family is here now."

Both sets of grandparents were smothered with hugs from all the children, even from Billy and Frankie who had only met them a few times before at church. "What a surprise! Frankie exclaimed. "Thanksgiving is going to be a whole lot of fun this year."

The two grandmothers joined Mrs. Fields in the kitchen to help with dinner preparations. Mr. Fields, the grandfathers, and the children continued to talk and watch the parade while the women cooked.

"Lunch time," Mrs. Fields entered the living room with a tray full of finger sandwiches for everyone. Grandma Fields followed carrying plates, forks, napkins, and a sack of assorted cold drinks. Grandma Cooper lagged behind with an assortment of chips and baked beans.

By this time the ballgame had started, and no one wanted to miss a second of the action. The lunch supplies were placed on the coffee table. "This is like a picnic," Frankie said.

"Yes, we thought you children might like picnicking in the living room," Grandma Cooper said. "Besides, there's not room at the kitchen table to sit with Grandma Fields getting ready to roll out her homemade dumplings. That takes up most of the table space."

"Dumplings, that sounds great!" Billy chimed as he filled his plate. "Our grandma used to make turkey and dumplings for us at Christmas time. Frankie and I both love dumplings. We like them fixed with chicken too."

"I've fixed them both ways," Grandma Fields said. "Your grandmother and I both learned to make dumplings at the same time from our grandmother, who would be your great-great grandmother."

"Mother, are you saying that Billy and Frankie are related to us?" Mr. Fields asked. "Why didn't you tell us?"

"Yes, Son, they are distant cousins." Grandma Fields said. "I thought you knew."

"Then they are family," Mr. Fields said. "I wondered why I felt a special bond with the children the moment I met them. What a surprise! Billy and Frankie, would you like to spend Christmas and New Year's week with us too while you're out of school?"

"Yes, please, that would be great!" Both children chimed simultaneously. Everyone laughed.

Thanksgiving passed with no more surprises. *What will happen during Christmas?* Mr. Fields wondered as he drove Billy and Frankie back to the orphanage. *Will Billy and Frankie like staying with us on a longer term basis? I want to adopt them.*

After Mr. Fields returned home he spoke with his wife about adopting Frankie and Billy. "You know, I was thinking the same thing," she said. "Let's start the process as soon as possible. Let's not tell any of the children though. We'll tell them at Christmas. I want them all to be surprised at the same time. Meanwhile, we'll have Billy and Frankie over and spend as much time with them as we can between now and Christmas."

Christmas approached. As the weeks passed, Billy and Frankie loved spending time with the Fields family. One evening while the children were having devotionals together, Frankie asked Billy, "Would you pray about something with me?"

"What do you want now? I guess you want another doll for Christmas," Billy replied as the children bowed their heads to pray.

"No, Billy, I don't want a doll. I want Mr. and Mrs. Fields to adopt us," Frankie said with tears in her eyes.

"I guess, that might be nice," Billy replied. He did not want Frankie being disappointed if such a large request did not come to pass.

# Fiction for the Children

School ended for Christmas break. The next day Mr. and Mrs. Fields picked up Billy and Frankie at the children's home to bring them to their home for the holidays. The children had passes to stay with the Fields family until school was to resume mid-January.

Christmas Eve everyone attended the Vespers Service at church. After church the Fields family joined the pastor and several other families in the congregation to deliver food boxes and Christmas gifts to less fortunate families in the community.

Although tired from the late night delivering gifts, all four children in the Fields home sprang out of bed early enthusiastic to open their Christmas gifts. Mr. and Mrs. Fields too were ready to spill the secret to the children that they planned to adopt Billy and Frankie. Two Christmas cards lay under the tree—one for Billy and Frankie to open together and one for Donna and Jerrod to open together. The parents planned to save the news for last. After all the other gifts were opened, they would have the children open their cards at the same time.

The moment came when all the presents had been unwrapped. "Children, we have another surprise for all of you," Mr. Fields said, as he directed all the children to sit on the couch. "We have a card for Billy and Frankie to open together, and another card for Donna and Jerrod to open together."

Inside Billy and Frankie's card was written, "Merry Christmas, and welcome to our family! You're here for good. We're adopting both of you. Is that okay with both of you?"

Donna and Jerrod's card read, "Merry Christmas, Children! Congratulations, you have a new brother and sister. Welcome Billy and Frankie to our family. We are adopting them."

Tears rolled down the cheeks of each child as they processed the news. Everyone cried and hugged as Billy said, "Frankie, our prayers were answered. We have a forever family now. Thank you, Jesus!"

No, Billy and Frankie did not return to the children's home to live. They visited once to get the rest of their belongings. Their friends at the home, they continued to see at school. The adoption was finalized within six months.

## Questions for Reflection

1. Why do you think Billy and Frankie were excited to be going to the Fields' home for Thanksgiving?
2. How were Donna and Jerrod surprised at Thanksgiving?
3. How do you think Billy and Frankie felt to find out they were related to the Fields family?
4. What does it mean to be adopted?
5. Why do you think Mr. and Mrs. Fields wanted to adopt Billy and Frankie?
6. Why do you think Mr. and Mrs. Fields wanted to wait until Christmas to tell the children about the adoption?
7. What is your favorite part of the story? Why?

## The following Scriptures are other Bible verses and how they apply to "A Forever Family":

| Scripture Reference: | Application: |
| --- | --- |
| John 6:11 | Saying grace before meals |
| 1 Timothy 5:8 | Mr. Fields wanting to adopt his cousins, the orphans |
| Luke 2: 1-20 | The biblical Christmas story |

# Sharing Jilts Jealousy

"Mom, isn't that Emma on the diving board?" ten year old Sharon asked her mother as they sunbathed by the shallow end of the Olympic sized swimming pool. "She told me she wasn't coming to the pool today."

Sharon's mother glanced from the book she was reading. "Yes, that does look like Emma. Isn't that Nancy, the new girl in our neighborhood, behind Emma on the diving board?"

"Probably so," Sharon said frowning. "They've been hanging out together. It's not fair. Emma was my best friend first."

"Sharon, I detect some jealousy in that statement. You shouldn't feel that way. A person can't have too many friends. You're being selfish. Go over there, and say 'hello' to the girls."

"Okay, Mom." Sharon jumped into the shallow end of the pool. "I'm going to swim over."

"Be careful, and tell the girls I said, 'hi'."

Sharon dove underwater to swim the length of the pool to the diving area. *The water feels so relaxing*, she thought. *I guess Emma likes Nancy better now than she does me.*

Sharon heard Emma's voice as she surfaced for a breathe of air. "Hi, Sharon."

"Hi, Emma. Is that Nancy with you?"

"Yes, she called and wanted me to come to the pool with her today. So I decided to change my plans from shopping with Mom to swimming with Nancy. I was swimming across the pool to say 'hello' to you and your mother. From the diving board, I spotted both of you lying in the sun."

"We saw you and Nancy on the boards. Mom said to tell you and Nancy 'hello'."

"Well, you tell her I said 'hello' also. Right now I need to get back to the diving end with Nancy. She doesn't swim as well so I promised her mother I'd watch her."

"How thoughtful," Sharon said. "Maybe we can get together another time."

"Okay, call me." Emma turned and dove underwater towards the deep end of the pool.

"Mom, Emma said to tell you 'hello'," Sharon said as she returned to lay on her new blue and gold stripped beach towel. *I wonder why Emma wouldn't change her plans for me but she did for Nancy*, she thought. *I feel like I've lost my best friend.*

"You weren't gone very long," Sharon's mother said as she laid her book aside. "That was fast swimming."

"Well, I met Emma halfway across the pool. She was on her way to speak to us. Mom, if Emma's mother approves, would you care to take Emma and me roller skating tomorrow night? We used to have fun whenever we went skating every week."

"Sure, you can call and ask her after dinner this evening.

"Hello, Emma. This is Sharon. Would you like to go skating tomorrow night like we used to do every week?"

"Oh, hi, Sharon. I just got home from the pool. I'm dripping water on mom's new carpet. May I call you later?"

"That's fine, Emma. I'm not going anywhere this evening."

An hour later the telephone rang as Sharon and her mother played a game of scrabble.

"That's probably Emma, Mom. Let me answer the phone."

"Sharon, this is Emma," Sharon heard through the receiver. "I wanted to call you back. I appreciate your inviting me to go skating tomorrow night. However, I have plans to spend the night with Nancy. Maybe another time."

"What happened to our friendship? I thought we were best friends; but now you do everything with Nancy."

"Don't be jealous, Sharon. Nancy's parents are divorcing. She's having a difficult time."

"Oh, I'm sorry. She didn't tell me that."

"I know. She was afraid you wouldn't identify with her struggles since your parents get along well. Whenever she heard about my parents' divorce, she opened up to me."

"I'm glad you can help her. Please forgive my jealousy."
"That's okay, Sharon. You and I are best friends."

## Questions for Reflection

1. Why was Sharon upset at Emma?
2. Why was Emma making an extra special effort to befriend Nancy? What did the girls have in common?
3. Why do you think Sharon's mother told her to go across the pool to speak to Emma and Nancy?
4. Why did Emma need to get back to Nancy in the deep end of the pool?
5. Emma and Nancy were left at the pool without an adult. Do you think this was safe, especially since Nancy did not swim very well?
6. When Emma turned down Sharon's invitation to go skating, what could Emma have done differently to keep Sharon from feeling left out?
7. Is there anyone in your class going through a bad time that you might help? Do you know someone you can help or encourage?

---

## The following Scriptures are other Bible verses and how they apply to "Sharing Jilts Jealousy":

| Scripture Reference: | Application: |
|---|---|
| Proverbs 14:30 | Jealousy |
| Luke 3:11; 2 Corinthians 8:13-15 | Sharing |
| Psalm 27:10 | God's caring for Emma and Nancy as children of divorce |

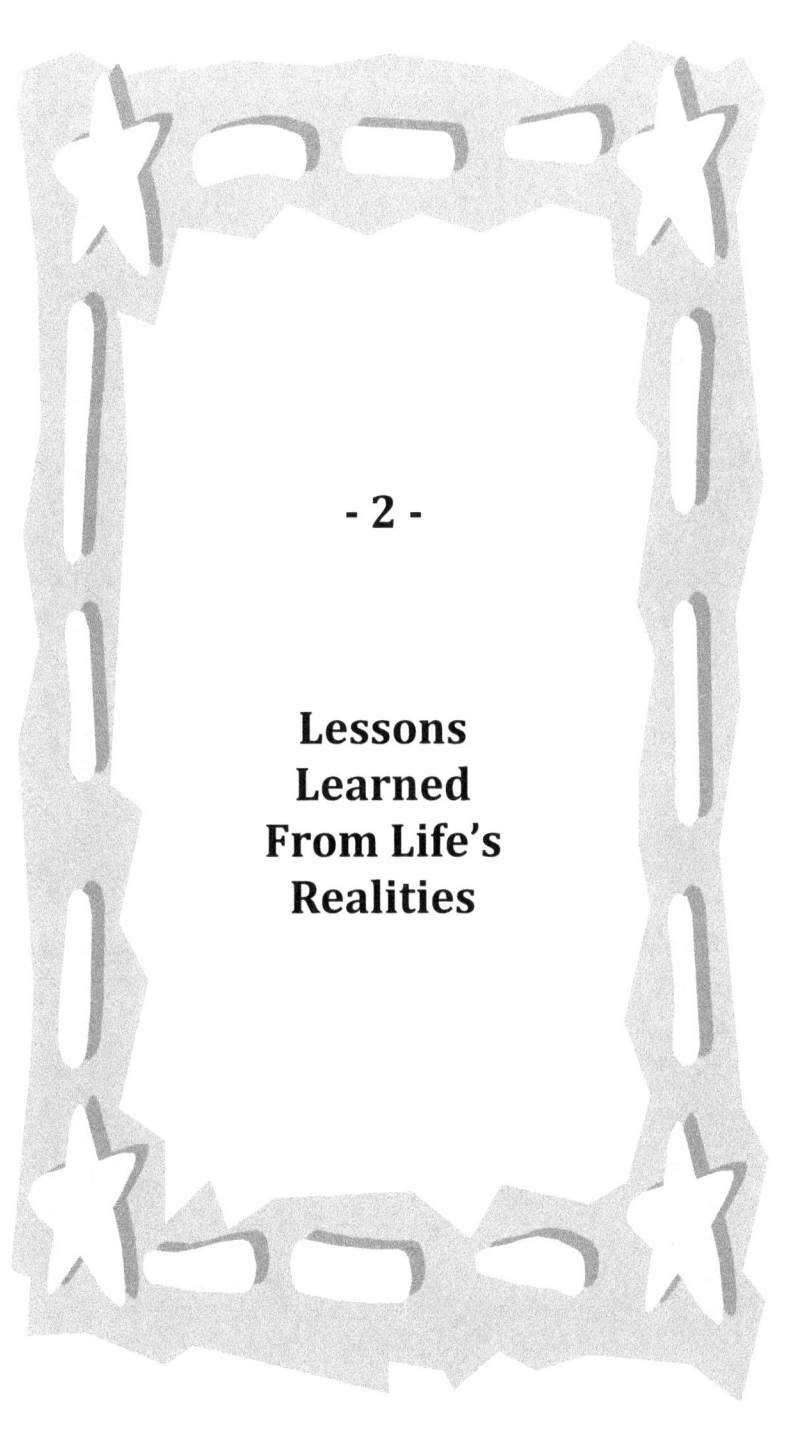

- 2 -

**Lessons
Learned
From Life's
Realities**

> "God is our refuge and strength, A very present help in trouble."
>
> Psalm 46:1

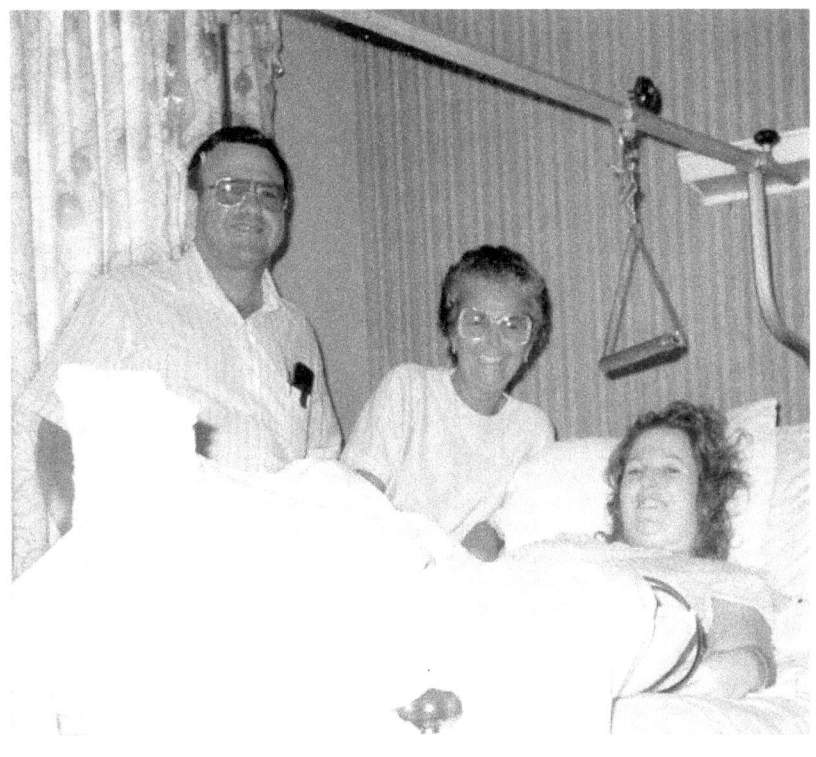

June 26, 1988—that day my life changed forever. This picture was taken during a visit from my parents not long after doctors had performed my first surgery July 6, 1988. During my first surgery a bone graph from my hip was performed and metal inserted to rebuild my ankle. Doctors removed the metal in a second surgery November 1989.

Dr. John H. Hoback, professor of chemistry, lectures to a class in the Science Building Auditorium.

Photo by Maria Dawson Broomes

Reprinted with permission from The Parthenon April 16, 1982 Marshall University.

## Handicapped? You Decide!

"Will you be able to walk? I hope you don't end up having to use a cane or something." This remark from a visiting deacon angered me as I lay in a hospital bed in 1988 following a fall down a flight of stairs that left me with a crushed left ankle.

*What's wrong with walking with a cane?* I thought as I heard this stranger's words. *I wish he would leave.*

"You might not walk again," Michael L. Reid, MD, orthopedic surgeon, said. "If you do walk, you might have a limp."

After Dr. Reid left my hospital room, I lay alone. *These people don't know me. I'll walk again. Even if I don't walk again, I know life isn't over*, I thought as I remembered Dr. Hoback's story.

"You wouldn't be worth two cents as a ditch digger, but with education the sky is the limit."

This was what a physician said to Dr. John H. Hoback whom I interviewed about his being the senior faculty member at Marshall University, Huntington, West Virginia in 1982. Dr. Hoback had been a victim of polio at the age of six.

When I first walked into Dr. Hoback's office without any forewarning of his physical limitations, I hesitated asking him about teaching from a wheelchair. Now years later only after experiencing an accident myself that could have left me in a wheelchair permanently, can I fully appreciate my meeting Dr. Hoback.

"Many people look at their weaknesses and get depressed. What they should do is find their strengths and develop them," Dr. Hoback said.

"They tell me I'm a cripple," said David Ring, born with cerebral palsy. "I'm a cripple; but, the Bible tells me I'm more than a conqueror through Christ Jesus who strengthens me."

"What's wrong with cerebral palsy?" David asks congregations with whom he shares his story of how God brought him from an insecure, grieving crippled boy to become a nationally-known evangelist with a wife and four healthy children. "The Bible says I was fearfully and wonderfully made by God. And God never says OOPS," David preaches. "They tell me it's a disability. It's a handicap. Baloney! Baloney! Baloney!"

For more about David's life, please see his website: www.davidring.org

"We often throw away broken things and underestimate God's power. But God uses broken people," David preaches. "When I am weak, then I am strong. They told me I'd never ride a bicycle, never drive a car, never finish college, never be a preacher, never make it into evangelism, never find a wife and would never father a child." David gives praise to God for having accomplished what in mankind's eyes would be impossible. "All I can say is to God be the glory. Great things He has done!"

"I've got cerebral palsy. What's your problem?" David Ring proclaims to congregations whenever he shares his testimony. David faced cerebral palsy's effects, the death of his parents at a young age and constant ridicule and discouragement from classmates and relatives. His story inspired me in 1989 when I was diagnosed with clinical depression, anxiety and an eating disorder.

*Why God? Why can't I live life like those around me whom I consider normal, or healthy?* I thought. Then I remembered something David Ring said:

# Lessons Learned from Life's Realities 67

"You know people come up to me and say 'Brother Dave, don't you want to be normal?' And I look at them. I say, 'What's normal?'"

Before meeting Dr. Hoback and David Ring, the life of my grandmother inspired me to achieve.

"Can't never could do anything," I remember my grandmother Earl S. Owens said. "Whenever a person says they can't, it usually means that person isn't willing to try."

No, my grandmother never had a newspaper article published about her nor did she ever make national television; but she left a legacy of perseverance and hope, regardless of the circumstances. This came from her stories of living through The Great Depression as a wife and mother; and, later, facing the consequences of being left a widow at a younger age than she or anyone else in her family then would have dreamed, or expected.

"He's my best friend," Mama said many times as we lay across her brown metal, queen-sized bed talking about God. "He'll be yours also." She was right. Now Jesus Christ is my greatest encouragement, comforter and counselor with my favorite Scripture II Timothy 1:7: "For God has not given us a spirit of fear; but of power and of love and of a sound mind."

By one definition, a handicap is a disadvantage. Reasoning from that perspective, any individual might wear the label "handicapped". If you disagree with this point, ask yourself: Do I know anyone who has an advantage over me in any area---more money, better physical health, stronger family support, etc.? We are all disadvantaged in one way at one point in time in comparison to another person.

Do disadvantages discourage you? Do you have negative circumstances you feel hinder you? Then look to the positive. Find your positive attributes. Build a dream based on your strengths.

Daily I am encouraged as I read these inspirational words on a magnet I keep on my refrigerator door: "Don't ever give up your dreams . . . and never leave them behind. Find them; make them yours, and all through your life, cherish them, and never let them go." Remembering, though, that dreams may change as one faces new challenges or obstacles in life. The key is in how we respond to new challenges or obstacles.

As a former pastor of mine, Dr. Jerry Sutton, former senior minister of Two Rivers Baptist Church, Nashville, Tennessee, said to me in a counseling session, "When we face problems or obstacles in life, they either make us bitter or better. You make the choice."

> "When we face problems or obstacles in life, they either make us bitter or better. You make the choice."

## Questions for Reflection

1. "You wouldn't be worth two cents as a ditch digger, but with education the sky is the limit." What do you think Dr. Hoback's doctor meant when he made this statement to him?
2. Some people limit God from working in their lives by listening to negative comments from others. Do you think this was the case with anyone mentioned in this story? Why or why not?
3. Given the definition, "a handicap is a disadvantage". What do you think are your handicaps? How do you handle them?
4. What does the author suggest you do when confronted with discouragement from others?
5. The author wrote that God is her biggest encourager. Who is your biggest encourager? Do you have others? How do they encourage you?
6. Many people in society feel fear or prejudice against others who are different. How do you feel and what do you do when you see a "handicapped" person, for example, in a wheelchair?
7. Who chooses whether we become bitter or better when faced with a trial in life?

## Yes, God Does Provide

"I wonder why Libby (fictitious) isn't here yet. She knows my video project is due. What'll we do if she doesn't come?" I said to Jenese, my talkative brunette roommate, and to Ken, our tall, blonde-headed friend. We arranged the six white dining chairs in a semicircle around the small dining room to prepare for the evening's scheduled group therapy session.

For over 10 years I'd wanted to pursue a master's degree in counseling. Now circumstances allowed me to follow this dream. I didn't want to blow my grade point average by not having my video presentation ready on time. The assignment was to produce a video facilitating a group of five to eight individuals in a therapeutic session over any topic that met the group members' needs or concerns. With each participant I invited to the session a Christian, I selected the topic "God's View Versus the World View: What's More Important?---Outward Appearance or Inward Character?".

"Don't worry, Pam," Ken said. "Just pray. You know God always provides. He won't let you down now."

"I know God will work out something."

"Maybe we can find a couple of neighbors outside who aren't busy," Jenese said. "Maybe they'd help you."

"I'll feed them dinner," I said.

"That should work," Ken said as he sat up the video stand.

"Libby was supposed to be here 15 minutes ago," I said frowning. "If she isn't here in another 15 minutes, let's go scan the neighborhood, Jenese."

While waiting for Libby's arrival, the group members present began to fill their stomachs with mouthwatering lasagna, garlic bread and finger foods that I had prepared earlier.

"Our country needs a revival," I said.

"Yes, we do," Ken said. "I believe revival is already starting to take place."

# Lessons Learned from Life's Realities

Jenese nodded her head in agreement.

When Libby hadn't arrived in 15 minutes, Jenese and I left to walk around the apartment complex in hopes of finding last minute recruits. *God, please help me find someone*, I prayed.

Two doors down a Latino man bent over the engine of a 1988 red Ford Mustang as I approached. *Maybe he'll take a break from his work if I offer him dinner*, I thought.

"Sir, would you mind taking a break for about 45 minutes to help me on an assignment for graduate school? I have to produce a video of me leading a group session. One of my scheduled participants didn't show," I said as I walked towards his car. With a pause, I added, "I'll feed you dinner."

"My wife is inside," the Latino said in a rich Spanish accent. "Ask her. She'll probably help you."

"Okay, thanks!" I ran to the apartment door. I knocked. A petite well-groomed Indian woman with long, thick dark curls answered the door.

"Ma'am, your husband told me to come ask you if you would mind doing me a favor," I said. "I'll feed both you and your husband dinner if you'll help me out."

"What would I need to do?" the woman asked.

"I'm leading a Biblically based group session for a graduate project. One of my scheduled participants did not come, nor call about not coming. Can you fill in for me?"

"Did you say it's Biblically based?" The woman paused. I nodded affirmatively. "Then we wouldn't be comfortable. We're Moslem."

"That's not a problem," I said. "I'd like getting your perspective on things."

"No, I'm sorry. We wouldn't be comfortable," the woman said as she closed the door.

*Oh, well, I struck out there*, I thought walking away. *I'll have to look further.*

"I found some help!" Jenese yelled as she ran towards me smiling. "I first went to an upstairs door. Whenever I knocked on the door, almost immediately a young handsome, black-headed, brown-eyed man opened the door. Instantly I smelled alcohol and cigarettes. I told the guy you needed someone to fill in for your group tonight.

'Miss, I'd be happy to help you,' he said. In fact, he said he'd love to help you; but he'd gotten company he didn't want to leave partying alone.

Then I came downstairs and went around the corner. I noticed a young poorly dressed, Caucasian couple sitting on the steps eating crab legs. I smiled as the thin, brown-eyed, brown-headed man and his slightly plump blue-eyed, red-headed companion smiled back.

'Hi, I'm Jenese. I live around the corner and down a couple of apartments. My roommate has a problem we hope you can help us with now. She has a video project group session due, and has had some last minute no-shows. Can you fill in for her? We have some dinner at our apartment you may also try---just for being our guests. Do you have 45 minutes of spare time to help?'

'What's the group about?' the young man asked.

'We'll be discussing God's view versus the world view on whether outward appearance or inward character is more important.'

'That sounds great! My name is Rod. This is Jennifer,' the young man said. 'We believe in Jesus Christ, His death, burial and resurrection. We'd love to help you---that's what we're here for, to serve others.'"

*This is wild*, I thought as Jenese finished her story. Rod and Jennifer walked around the corner of the red brick building towards our apartment. With Rod's long shoulder length greasy hair, his old tattered blue jeans with a hole in the knee and with Jennifer's poor, unkempt appearance, I would have stereotyped these two people as a couple of "junkies", not as Christians professing Jesus Christ as Lord and Savior. *This is going to be an interesting evening*, I thought. *God has a lesson in this for me. If Jenese hadn't invited them, I sure wouldn't want them in the video. I hope their appearance doesn't hurt my grade.*

> "In like manner also, that the women adorn themselves in modest apparel, with propriety and moderation, not with braided hair or gold or pearls or costly clothing, but, which is proper for women professing godliness, with good works" (I Tim. 2:9-10). This key verse was used as the springboard for the group discussion "God's View Versus the World View: What's More Important--Outward Appearance or Inward Beauty?" Unanimously we agreed that inward character should be valued over outward appearance.

## Questions for Reflection

1. What's more important to you—outward appearance or inward beauty (character)? Why?
2. Why do you think the author was upset at Libby's being late? Is it ever okay to be late for an appointment?
3. There is an old saying, "Where God guides, He provides". Is this statement biblical? How does this statement apply to this story?
4. Why do you think the author initially only invited Christians to be in the group?
5. Why do you think the Indian woman did not want to help the author by being in the group discussion?
6. How was Christ reflected through Ken and Jenese in the story?
7. Why do think the author initially would not have wanted Rod and Jennifer to be in the video?

## God Knows Best

"Don't date anyone you wouldn't want to be married to at that point in time," I remember my grandmother said. "You never know who you'll fall in love with. If you don't want to live with someone who smokes, don't date anyone who smokes. If you don't want a husband who drinks, don't date guys who drink. The Bible says for Christians not to be unequally yoked to unbelievers."

. . . words I wish I'd taken heed to in early 1994 when I first met Gary.

Gary and I met at the bus stop on the corner of Lebanon Road and McGavock Pike in Nashville, Tennessee. I was on my way home with groceries from Kroger's.

"Do you like country music?" a tall brown-eyed, brown-headed man said. "I noticed the Keith Whitley T-shirt you're wearing."

*He's cute*, I thought. "Keith was my cousin. That's why I wear this shirt. I listen mostly to Gospel music. However, I do like country music, especially Keith's."

"I sing and play country music," the man said. "Keith was one of my favorite entertainers."

"Really?" I said. "What's your name?"

"Gary. What's your name?"

"Pam," I said as I tried to hide my excitement thinking, *he seems like a nice guy. He's attractive.*

"Are you a Christian?" *Gary's answer to this question will determine the direction of this conversation*, I thought. *If he's not a Christian, then I'll witness to him. Maybe I should invite him to the single's party I'm having this weekend at my apartment.*

"Yes, I am," Gary assured me.

"I attend Two Rivers Baptist Church. Do you attend church anywhere?"

"No, I'm new in town."

*I need to invite him to my party*, I thought. "You're new in town. Where's your hometown?"

"West Virginia," he said smiling.

"Really? I graduated from Marshall University in Huntington."

"Would you go out with me?" Gary winked at me.

"I don't know," I replied. "I don't go out with men until we're friends first. I'm having a Christian singles' party at my place this weekend. Why don't you come to my party? You'd get to meet a lot of nice Christian singles in town."

"I don't know," he said. "I'm not much on being in big crowds. May I call you?"

"Sure," I said pulling out a piece of paper and pen from my purse to write down my telephone number. "Here's my number."

"Thanks, Pam." Gary smiled and winked at me.

"Call me later, Gary. Here comes the bus." *I wonder if he'll call*, I thought as I stepped into the bus. *He's good looking, and he said he's a Christian.*

As I prepared snacks for the upcoming party, the telephone rang.

"Hello." I checked the time so I wouldn't burn the brownies baking in the oven, or overcook the eggs I planned to devil.

"Hello. Is this Pam?"

"Yes, this is Pam. Who is this?"

"This is Gary. Remember from the bus stop?"

"Oh, yes. Hi. I wondered whether you'd call?"

"You were nice to me."

"Well, I try to be a good witness." I smiled to myself. "Have you given any thought to coming to my party?"

"I don't know. There's something you need to know."

"What's that?" I said as I heard a lot of music over the telephone. *He sounds drunk*, I thought.

"I'm an alcoholic. That's why I came to Nashville . . . to get treatment."

# Lessons Learned from Life's Realities          77

*This guy needs friends*, I thought. *Maybe I can get him in with guys from church who used to drink. They might be able to help him.*

"Sounds like you could use some friends," I said. "I think you should come to my party."

"I'd be uncomfortable since I wouldn't know anyone else. You're right saying I need friends. You can be my friend."

"Well, right now I have to go finish deviling eggs. If you want to come to my party, come. If not, I understand. Bye."

"I met this great looking guy at the bus stop the other day," I said to Bobbie, my best friend and the first to arrive for the singles' party at my apartment. "He seems like a nice guy."

"Really!" Bobbie said. "Is he coming tonight?"

"I don't know. I invited him. He said he probably wouldn't come because he didn't know anyone. He needs friends though. He said he came to Nashville for treatment to overcome an alcohol problem."

"Don't get involved," warned Bobbie. "Believe me, once an alcoholic, always an alcoholic. I know. I was married to one."

"Well, the guy needs friends," I said. "Somebody needs to minister to him."

"You don't know what you're getting into," Bobbie cautioned me.

The next day Gary called. *What am I going to do if he asks me to go out again*, I thought. *Bobbie made good points. However, I also know alcoholism might be an illness. I wouldn't want someone holding my chemical imbalance against me. Maybe I can help him.*

"I'm sorry I didn't make it for your party," Gary said. "I'd like for us to be friends. Will you go out with me? Or could we meet somewhere?"

"I guess we can be friends . . . but, just friends," I said. "I'd be more comfortable if we met at a restaurant somewhere."

"Where do you want to meet?"

"Do you like pizza?" I said as I thought, *I've got to be careful not to jump into something with him too fast.*

"Sure, I eat pizza."

"Okay. How about us meeting at the Pizza Hut in Donelson near the bus stop where we met?"

"That sounds good," Gary said. "But will you let me pick up your tab?"

"Only if this is a gesture of friendship," I said as I thought, *he's my kind of man---one that believes a man should pay a woman's way whenever they go out.*

"What's your favorite kind of pizza?" Gary asked as we sat in Pizza Hut.

"Sausage and pepperoni," I said.

"Then that's what we'll order." Gary lit a cigarette.

"Oh, I didn't know you smoked," I said. "I don't smoke, and I don't allow anyone to smoke in my home."

"Oh, I wouldn't smoke in your place," he said. "Mom always made me go outside whenever I smoked at her house."

"Why don't you quit?" I said as Gary puffed on his cigarette. "Smoking is a nasty habit."

"I'll quit for you," he said.

"His smoking is another red flag for you," Bobbie said the next Sunday whenever we talked about Gary and I meeting at Pizza Hut. "I don't want to see you hurt."

"He said he'd quit drinking and smoking. He also said he'd go to church with me."

"That's what they'll all say until they get you," Bobbie said.

Now looking back after Gary's and my annulment in 1995 and before marrying Milton, I realized the importance of paying attention to red flags in relationships. When God said in II Corinthians 6:14, "Do not be unequally yoked with unbelievers. For what fellowship has righteousness with lawlessness? And what communion has light with darkness?", I began applying this Scripture to every area of my life. I learned to either back out of a relationship with red flags, or I would establish healthier boundaries within that relationship. That's because I finally understood God knows best. He certainly gave me the best when He sent Milton into my life.

# Lessons Learned from Life's Realities

## Questions for Reflection

1. What was the author's grandmother's advice about dating?
2. Do you think the author was wrong to invite Gary to the church singles party at her home? Why or why not?
3. Bobbie made the statement, "Believe me, once an alcoholic, always an alcoholic." Is this statement correct biblically? (See 1 Corinthians 6:10-11.)
4. The author ignored a lot of red flags in her relationship with Gary initially hoping she could minister to him. What do you think went wrong? (See James 1:14.)
5. The author does not allow anyone to smoke in her home. Do you think she is wrong? What does God's Word say about smoking? (See 1 Corinthians 3:17 and 1 Peter 5:8.)
6. Gary told the author he was a Christian. Yet he did not live by God's commands. What does the Bible say about that? (See 1 John 2:4.)
7. What do you think you would do if you met someone like Gary on the street?

## Put Unjust Bias to Death

An all white church . . . An all white school . . . And an all white community . . . Places where I thrived as a child. Little did I realize the prejudice created in me from my lack of exposure to; lack of knowledge about; and, lack of understanding of other cultures until I faced the culture shock of moving from small town Ashland, Kentucky to Nashville, Tennessee.

Sure, I studied about racial prejudice manifested in history in the form of the Holocaust, slavery and other racially biased evils. Not until I experienced having to ride buses with, and having to work side by side with individuals of other races did I recognize how prejudice had crept into my life out of ignorance.

"Besides a couple of managers, I'm the only white employee at work," I said to family members and friends after I agreed to work at a fast food restaurant until I could find a professional position where I could use my college education. *This makes me uncomfortable*, I thought. *I don't like being the minority*.

Later I realized prejudice goes deeper than the color of a person's skin. Handicapped persons often experience prejudice. In fact, any difference in another person that makes one uncomfortable can result in prejudice. Or, at least, I recognize this temptation within myself.

Differences in physical appearance and mental abilities create conflict within me. With a shorter, fatter stature as a child, how often do you think I was selected first in physical education class to be on a classmate's sports team? Never.

"Men don't like chubby women," I heard my entire childhood. True, some men don't. However, men do exist who value women for who they are as a person, not for physical attractiveness alone. However, because I believed this false premise, I rarely had boyfriends growing up. *Besides, what guy would want to date a girl who made better grades than him?* I thought.

Before an ordeal with a crushed ankle, I used to shun anyone in a wheelchair or with any type of physical handicap. My prejudice stemmed from a fear, or insecurity about not knowing what to say when face to face with the physically handicapped. I remember my aunt had a friend with a handicapped child we used to visit whenever I was in elementary school. *I can't wait until we leave here*, I thought as my family spoke with this individual as I tried to sit in a corner as far out of the picture as possible.

Not only have I noticed physical and mental differences within myself and others creating prejudice and confusion, but I have known of differences in lifestyles and socioeconomic levels leading to prejudice. I remember children at my elementary and junior high schools from affluent families snubbing children from families of a lower economic level. Most of the time, the poorer students financially also were the poorer students academically. Thus, these children got a double dose of prejudice: first, from being labeled "poor"; and, secondly, from being labeled "dumb". Personally, I took my academic gifts for granted without thinking about the disadvantages the poorer children faced. Not until I was in high school, did I begin helping other students with homework and studying for exams.

"Mom says our church is the only one that goes by what the Bible says," I remember a classmate who attended a different church saying during lunch once whenever I was in elementary school.

"What church you attend doesn't matter," I said, "as long as you're saved." At that time, my naiveté and her criticizing my family's faith prompted me to rebuke her.

"You're wrong," this classmate said to me and a friend, who also attended the same church my family attended.

"No, I'm not either," I said. "What your denomination is doesn't matter. What's important is what's in your heart."

"Don't argue with her," my friend said. "Mom said we shouldn't argue about religion."

I expect religious bias outside of the Christian faith. After all, Jesus said, "I am the way, the truth, and the life. No one comes to the Father except through Me" (John 14:6). A Christian should want to share Christ with others who think they can come to God through Buddha, Mohammed or any means other than salvation through Jesus Christ. At least, that's my desire. I wouldn't want anyone going to hell because I failed to follow Christ's command to share the Gospel.

On the other hand, "Of all the armies in existence, the Christian army is the only army that shoots it's own wounded," I heard someone say years ago. Prejudice between Christian denominations hurts the faith, and displeases God. "Have we not all one father? Has not one God created us? Why do we deal treacherously with one another . . ." (Malachi 2:10).

Prejudice against different denominational worship practices and traditions runs rampant. "If you don't belong to my church, you won't go to Heaven," type attitudes need to be discarded. After all, does God look at what type worship service you attend, or does He look at what's in your heart? Does God judge us by whether we sing with or without musical instruments? How concerned is God over whether families sit together in church, or whether the men want to sit on one side of the building with the women sitting on the opposite side of the church? Is criticizing Christians with different traditions worth the risk of being a hindrance to some lost soul who sees confusion and criticism, rather than love, between Christian denominations? No wonder lost people seek false gods.

What we need to be reminded is that being different does not imply inferiority or superiority among the Christian faith. Different is different---not better, or worse. Respect for our fellow brothers and sisters in Christ needs to be practiced, and taught to younger children.

Prejudice resulting from denominational differences, different socioeconomic levels, different physical attributes and different abilities should be replaced with love and respect. If someone's behavior or beliefs are contrary to the Scriptures, then I'll be the first to support your prejudice. Otherwise, let prejudice die. "I charge you before God and the Lord Jesus Christ and the elect angels that you observe these things without prejudice, doing nothing with partiality" (I Timothy 5:21).

> "If My people who are called by My name will humble themselves, and pray and seek My face, and turn from their wicked ways, then I will hear from heaven, and will forgive their sin and heal their land."
>
> II Chronicles 7:14

## Questions for Reflection

1. "Men don't like chubby women." This statement is a stereotype. If the statement were true, how does God feel about chubby women? (See 1 Samuel 16:7.)
2. The author grew up with a lot of racial prejudice. What does God say about the different races? (See Romans 10:12.)
3. The author mentions prejudice based on socioeconomic level. What does God's Word say about this type of prejudice? (See Proverbs 22:2.)
4. Many people believe that if a person does not belong to a specific denomination, then that person can not be a Christian and go to Heaven. What does God's Word say? (See Acts 10:34-43.)
5. Gangs and bullying in today's society stem from personal prejudices. What does God's Word say we should do when faced with a gang or bully? (See Proverbs 1:10; 4:14-17.)
6. Discrimination is rooted in prejudice. Have you ever been discriminated against for some reason? What did you do?
7. Many Christians are persecuted in today's world due to religious prejudice. What does the Scripture say about Christian persecution? (See 1 John 3:13; Matthew 5:10-12; 1 Peter 3:14-15.)

# Ground Gossip

"She's been telling everyone you're crazy. She's been telling everybody that you tried to kill yourself," a friend said whenever I returned to church after receiving treatment in Tennessee Christian Medical Center's stress unit for depression.

"That's none of her concern," I said. "What gives her the right to tell everyone my business?"

"Just consider the source," my friend said.

"I know. She's a gossip. Her big mouth never stops. She's hurt any chance I might've had with a couple of new men who visited here. You can't let her know whom you'd like to date. She'll scare them off. She also exaggerates everything; thus, a lot of what she says isn't true."

Gossip . . . idle talk and rumors, especially about the private affairs of others, according to Webster's New World Dictionary of the American Language, Second College Edition. Show me a person who says he or she has never gossiped, and I'll show you a liar. I don't know anyone whom I haven't heard gossip about someone at least once.

Remember the game teachers used to play in class in elementary school. You know the one where the teacher tells a secret to the first person in the first row of the classroom. That student in turn shares the secret with the student behind him, and on around the room until every child has heard the secret. By the time the secret gets back to the teacher, how often does she hear the same message?

"Sticks and stones may break my bones, but words can never hurt me." How often did you hear this statement repeated as a child? Is there any truth to this old wives' tale?

"The words of a talebearer are as wounds, and they go down into the innermost parts of the belly" (Proverbs 18:8, KJV). For this reason, before you share information with others, I recommend you consider both the source of the information and the recipient of the information.

The first questions I like to ask myself before repeating information revolve around the source. Can I prove the validity of the information? How reliable is the source? Do I know the source as a gossip? If not, how reliable is my source's source of information? If you have any doubt about the credibility of the information or the source's credibility, repeating the information might result in trouble. For example, I remember a minister rebuking me about something I had shared with someone.

"Well, that's what I heard," was my excuse.

"That's gossip," the minister said. "You shouldn't have repeated it. Can you prove what you heard?"

"No." I shook my head from side to side.

"Then, I suggest the next time you hear something like that about someone, and if what you hear bothers you that much, go directly to that person and confront them with what you hear. Let gossip stop with you."

The credibility of the recipients to what you say is as important as the source of your information. Ask yourself: Are the people I'm about to share with trustworthy? Are they gossips? Or do they make mountains out of mole hills whenever they repeat something?

"He who goes about as a talebearer reveals secrets; Therefore do not associate with one who flatters with his lips" (Proverbs 20:19). This verse is one I wish I had been aware of several years ago before I made a remark to a person I knew had a reputation for being a gossip. The situation almost resulted in my loosing a friend.

"She said you said you wanted to marry me," I remember a new male acquaintance saying to me as I lay in a hospital bed after I crushed my left ankle.

"I'm lying here not knowing whether I'll walk again," I said, "and, she's causing me this trouble. I don't need this!"

"I'm sorry. That's what she told me; so, I wanted to set things straight."

"Well, I never said that. What I said was that I liked you. You seemed like a nice guy to have as a friend. Friendship is the only thing I want from you. She blew an innocent remark out of proportion."

"Okay," he said. "I'm sorry. I know you don't need this stress now. We'll be friends."

Another final question I think anyone should consider before repeating information to another person is crucial. Even if the source is accurate; and, if the person I'm sharing with is trustworthy, would I want someone sharing this information about me? Sharing secrets and having personal conversations occurs among circles of friends. However, within several group discussions that I have witnessed, the conversations turned into "gossip sessions", under the guise of sharing prayer requests. I have been in more than one prayer circle that ended up being a "gossip session" before any of the group members realized what was happening.

Several years ago I made the conscious decision not to choose individuals, with reputations as being "gossips", as my closest friends. I decided if I got caught in a situation where people are gossiping, I would either leave the setting or confront the group about the situation. For example, I remember the following account happening a few months ago whenever I was having lunch with a group of friends from where I worked.

"Do you realize we're sitting here gossiping?" I said frowning at my friends. "I'm not comfortable with this conversation."

"I agree with Pam," Muriel said.

"We shouldn't be talking about this with the others here," Harriette said. "They're not in our department. Let's change the subject."

The idle chatter continued. Muriel left the table.

"I have to get back to work," I said rising from my chair.

If you get caught riding in a car, for example, where other individuals are gossiping, then you cannot leave the setting. In that case, I first recommend that you ask the other passengers politely not to gossip. If they continue, then pray quietly to yourself for the ones gossiping and for the victims of the gossip.

The Scriptures are clear about what God thinks about gossiping. "You shall not go about as a talebearer among your people . . ." (Leviticus 19:16).

Before you spread that next rumor you hear, think about how you might hurt both yourself and the one being talked about. Remember, "A talebearer reveals secrets, But he who is of a faithful spirit conceals a matter" (Proverbs 11:13), and "He who covers a transgression seeks love, But he who repeats a matter separates friends" (Proverbs 17:9).

## Questions for Reflection

1. How do you think the author felt when she learned others were gossiping about her depression and attempted suicide?
2. "Suicide is a permanent solution to a temporary problem." Now recovered from depression the author and other mental health professionals often make the previous statement to those who are depressed and not wanting to live. How do you think God feels about suicide? (See Ecclesiastes 7:17 and 2 Corinthians 12:9.)
3. Do you know what to do if you or someone you know is feeling depressed or suicidal? (The answer: Tell someone, and get professional help like the author got to overcome the trials in her life.)
4. "Sticks and stones may break my bones, but words can never hurt me." What do you think this statement means? Do you think the statement is true?
5. What are three factors the author recommends be considered before sharing information with anyone? Why are these factors important?
6. In today's churches "prayer groups" can quickly become "gossip sessions". How do you think this can be avoided?
7. What should you do when caught in a situation where people are gossiping?

# Wipe out Worry

"A person who says they never worried about anything, never loved anybody," my grandmother said frequently. One of my grandmother's few misconceptions contributed to developing an unhealthy habit in me.

"I couldn't sleep last night for thinking about the test," I said on the day of an exam in high school.

"Don't worry," a friend said. "You'll do okay."

"I hope so," I said reviewing my study notes.

"You always worry. But then you do better than the rest of us on the test."

About 20 years later I sat in the Nashville office of psychiatrist Gilbert W. Raulston, MD.

"Do you worry a lot?" Dr. Raulston asked as he made notes on my chart.

"Yes, I do."

"How does it affect you?"

"Oh, I can't sleep. I also have a lot of stomach problems. I have reflux."

"Okay." The doctor looked up from his notes. "Do other members of your family worry a lot?"

"What's that got to do with it?" I said. "I was diagnosed with anxiety disorder."

"That's part of it," Dr. Raulston said as he continued to make notes. "Worry also is learned in families."

"Yes, I guess I did develop the problem honestly. A lot of people in my family worries."

To be worried is to feel distressed in the mind; be anxious, troubled or uneasy, according to Webster's New World Dictionary of the American Language, Second College Edition. What happens when an individual worries? I found two disadvantages of worry in the Scriptures: unfruitfulness and a shorter life span.

# Lessons Learned from Life's Realities

"Now he who received seed among the thorns is he who hears the word, and the cares of this world and the deceitfulness of riches choke the word, and he becomes unfruitful" (Matthew 13:22). For example, I remember a few times when I wasn't able to go to work because of losing sleep from worrying about an uncontrollable situation the night before. At other times, I went to work after a restless night of worrying. What happened? My productivity for that day was less than my normal performance.

"Which of you by worrying can add one cubit to his stature" (Matthew 6:27)?

> Worry and anxiety are related to the length of one's life in the phrase add one cubit unto his stature. A cubit is a measurement of about eighteen inches. However, this reference is probably not to one's actual height but to the length of his life. The term "stature" (Gr helikia) may in this place mean "age." Thus the idea seems to be that a man cannot add the smallest measure to the span of his life by worrying. In fact, modern medicine would tell us that worry actually shortens one's life. (Falwell, J., 1997, c1994, Worry or anxiety, KJV Bible Commentary [computer file], electronic ed., Logos Library System, Nashville: Thomas Nelson)

A person who worries excessively and unrealistically for a period of at least 6 months might need treatment for an anxiety disorder. Generalized anxiety disorder is a medical illness where individuals with the disorder experience trembling, muscular aches or soreness, restlessness, insomnia, sweating, abdominal upsets, dizziness, concentration problems, edginess and irritability.

Contentment is the opposite of worry. Besides avoiding the health problems associated with being a chronic worrier, does freedom from worry or anxiety have other benefits? Let's see what God's Word says about worry and contentment.

> Be anxious for nothing, but in everything by prayer and supplication, with thanksgiving, let your requests be made known to God; and the peace of God, which surpasses all

understanding, will guard your hearts and minds through Christ Jesus. (Philippians 4:6-7)

In my personal experiences I have found greater productivity results as a by product on whatever I am doing whenever I am content. When I am at peace, I sleep better; thus, I have more energy to do the best work possible. Whenever I am more productive in life, I receive more blessings in life. For example, self-satisfaction and compliments from supervisors have been by products on more productive days.
My personal experience is supported by God's Word:

Blessed is the man who trusts in the Lord, And whose hope is the Lord. For he shall be like a tree planted by the waters, Which spreads out its roots by the river, And will not fear when heat comes; But its leaf will be green, And will not be anxious in the year of drought, Nor will cease from yielding fruit. (Jeremiah 17:7-8)

"You didn't become a worrier over night," psychologist Kathryn B. Sherrod Ph.D. said during one of our therapy sessions several years ago. "Breaking the habit will take some time. I suggest you set aside a designated amount of time each day that you allow yourself time to worry, and only allow yourself to worry during that time. Gradually cut back on the amount of time you give yourself to worry."
"That sounds weird to me."
"Journaling your worries also might help," Dr. Sherrod said noting my chart. "A lot of my patients like to write out whatever is bothering them."
"Yes, writing is a good way to relieve stress." I nodded to agree with Dr. Sherrod. "I have a recovery notebook from where I went through therapy before. My therapist then used to give me a writing assignment at the end of each session to work on between sessions."

Another alternative to worrying about a problem or situation is to react with concern. What is the difference between a worried person and a concerned person? Where a worrier often dwells on a situation to the point of obsession, a concerned person thinks or prays the matter through, and then moves on with life. While a worrier imagines the worst case scenario, a concerned person looks for a positive solution. Here is an example of where I acted out of concern:

"Hi, Jennifer. My name is Pam Owens." I said to Jennifer Cooke of Cottage Cove Ministries, an inner city outreach to the residents, especially children, in the Vine Hill community of Nashville. " I heard you need help getting together a Christmas party for the children there."

"Yes, that's true," Jennifer said.

"Well, I have a background in public relations, and my passion is to serve children. I'd like to help."

"That's great," Jennifer said.

Rather than jumping in to offer my assistance to the Cottage Cove staff, I could have sat around worrying about what they were going to do for help; or, I could have complained to other individuals without my educational background who weren't as qualified to take on the responsibility. Instead, I served as the coordinator, the liaison between the Cottage Cove staff and the singles from my home church who agreed to sponsor the Christmas party that year.

As an alternative to worrying, besides praying, weaning yourself off of worry, keeping a worry journal and offering positive solutions, try relaxing yourself through exercise or another activity you enjoy. This helps to distract your mind from whatever is bothering you.

The key in breaking my worry habit was recognizing worry as a sin. I repented and asked for God's help in winning the war over worry. By being obedient to the Scripture, "Therefore humble yourselves under the mighty hand of God, that He may exalt you in due time, casting all your care upon Him, for He cares for you" (I Peter 5:6-7)., I worry less and have fewer health problems. My trust and faith are in Jesus Christ.

"I can do all things through Christ who strengthens me" (Philippians 4:13).

## Questions for Reflection

1. What are two disadvantages to worry found in the Scriptures?
2. What are health affects to worrying?
3. What are ways to overcome the habit and sin of worrying?
4. The author now considers worry a generational sin (See Numbers 14:18.) in her family that she learned and was able to overcome. Do you think you have any generational sins in your life? Other examples might be overeating or eating unhealthy.
5. What was the key for the author in breaking her worry habit?
6. What is the difference between a worried person and a concerned person?
7. Faith is often given as the opposite to worry. What does having faith mean to you?

## Cease Slothfulness

"Do your homework as soon as you get home from school. Homework comes before television, playing outside and anything else." . . . One of my parents' rules both parents said many times. Not only did my parents adopt this policy for my brother and me; but, they never reneged on the enforcement of what was to be my priority during the school year. For example:

"Dad, may I go outside and ride my bicycle?" I said one evening after getting home from elementary school.

"Have you finished your homework?" Dad said as he glanced at me from the newspaper he was reading.

"No, I've started my assignments; but, I'm not finished."

"Finish your homework first."

"But it'll be dark then. I can't ride my bike after dark," I said. *I hope he lets me ride my bike*, I thought.

"You know the rule. Homework first."

"Okay," I said. I headed towards my bedroom where I did my homework.

Through the years, my parents' strict enforcement of their homework policy reaped many rewards. For example, I served as a member of the National Honor Society in both junior high and high school. Later, I graduated Co-Salutatorian winning numerous academic awards. Over the years with my parents' guidance, I learned how to be responsible and I adopted a strong personal work ethic.

"Pamela can't touch her toes in physical education class but only giggles about it," Mrs. Martha Holmes, my first grade teacher, wrote to my parents in my first report card. After over 40 years, I still cannot touch my toes as well as I would want. Thus, indicating exercising as the one area in life where I have a tendency to be lazy.

What does the Bible say about laziness? "Because of laziness the building decays, And through idleness of hands the house leaks" (Ecclesiastes 10:18). Applying this to my exercise regimen, whenever I do not walk and work out consistently with my stress and anxiety reducing exercise video, then I have less energy, my clothes fit tighter and I do not sleep as well. On the other hand, whenever I am exercising daily, I have more energy, I sleep better and I reap the numerous other benefits of exercise, including weight loss (or, at least, weight maintenance), lower cholesterol and triglyceride levels and a stronger cardiovascular system.

What are possible consequences to laziness? The first by product of laziness I think of might be hunger. For example, if a person is too lazy to maintain employment, then he would not have money to buy healthy foods. II Thessalonians 3:10 says "For even when we were with you, we commanded you this: If anyone will not work, neither shall he eat." Financial ruin, perhaps even poverty, also may result. "He who has a slack hand becomes poor, But the hand of the diligent makes rich" (Proverbs 10:4).

Shame and embarrassment can be consequences of laziness. Whenever I am unemployed, I feel embarrassed having to ask others for financial assistance. Other family members and friends are affected by one's laziness. "He who gathers in summer is a wise son; He who sleeps in harvest is a son who causes shame" (Proverbs 10:5).

A lazy person might be greedy. "The desire of the lazy man kills him, For his hands refuse to labor. He covets greedily all day long, But the righteous gives and does not spare" (Proverbs 21:25-26).

"He who is slothful in his work Is a brother to him who is a great destroyer" (Proverbs 18:9). I understand the truth behind that verse: A lazy person is unproductive, and wastes time and whatever talents God has given him just like a destructive person. "The soul of a lazy man desires, and has nothing; . . ." (Proverbs 13:4). How much spiritual growth do you think occurs in a person with a lazy disposition?

Lazy individuals can end up in bondage. "The hand of the diligent will bear rule: but the slothful shall be under tribute" (Proverbs 12:24, KJV).

Diligence is the opposite of laziness. The Scriptures are clear about the benefits of being diligent. Profit and financial security are obvious consequences of working diligently. "The plans of the diligent lead surely to plenty, But those of everyone who is hasty, surely to poverty" (Proverbs 21:5).

Whenever I am diligent about exercising, I remain at peace with myself. When I neglect exercise, I feel guilty. This personal observation is supported by Scripture: "Therefore, beloved, looking forward to these things, be diligent to be found by Him in peace, without spot and blameless" (II Peter 3:14).

A diligent worker is an obedient worker. "Be diligent to present yourself approved to God, a worker who does not need to be ashamed, rightly dividing the word of truth" (II Timothy 2:15). Spiritual growth also results from diligence. " . . . But the soul of the diligent shall be made rich" (Proverbs 13:4).

> For God is not unjust to forget your work and labor of love which you have shown toward His name, in that you have ministered to the saints, and do minister. And we desire that each one of you show the same diligence to the full assurance of hope until the end, that you do not become sluggish, but imitate those who through faith and patience inherit the promises. For when God made a promise to Abraham, because He could swear by no one greater, He swore by Himself, saying, "Surely blessing I will bless you, and multiplying I will multiply you." (Hebrews 6:10-14)

Why should a person work? I found three reasons in the Bible: to take care of your possessions, to provide for your family and to help others. "Let us therefore be diligent to enter that rest, lest anyone fall according to the same example of disobedience" (Hebrews 4:11).

"Be diligent to know the state of your flocks, and attend to your herds" (Proverbs 27:23). Applying this to modern day society,

I believe we need to take care of our homes, cars and the rest of the environment.

God's displeasure with a person who does not provide for his family is enough motive for me to work. "But if anyone does not provide for his own, and especially for those of his household, he has denied the faith and is worse than an unbeliever" (I Timothy 5:8).

Being in a position that allows me to serve others always results in a blessing for me. For example, I remember a six year old girl named Tabitha who used to be my neighbor.

"Tabitha, do you want to go to church with me next Sunday. Next Sunday is Easter." I asked her as I drove us home from church.

"No, I don't think so," Tabitha said frowning.

"Why, Tabitha?" I said as I continued to drive. "You always have so much fun in Sunday school."

"All the other children will have new outfits. I don't want to wear my tennis shoes on Easter."

"Don't worry, Tabitha. Let me talk to your mother."

"Tabitha said she doesn't want to go to Easter services because she won't have a new outfit," I said to Tabitha's mother. "Are you going to buy her a new outfit for next week?"

"I can't afford a new dress, new shoes and everything else she needs. I saw a dress the other day I wanted to buy her."

"Well, how about if I buy her new shoes and a pair of tights? I don't make a whole lot of money either. However, I can afford that. Then you can buy that dress. Will that work?"

"Sure, thanks, Pam," Tabitha's mother said smiling. "I'm glad Tabitha can go with you next Sunday without feeling embarrassed by her clothes."

Seeing the joy and excitement in Tabitha's face over getting a new pair of shoes was blessing enough for me. What can you do today to help someone?

God's Word tells us, "I have shown you in every way, by laboring like this, that you must support the weak. And remember the words of the Lord Jesus, that He said, 'It is more blessed to give than to receive'" (Acts 20:35).

Being diligent requires effort and sacrifice. Sometimes I get tired when I work. Then I remember the Scripture: "And let us not grow weary while doing good, for in due season we shall reap if we do not lose heart" (Galatians 6:9).

## Questions for Reflection

1. Although the author did not always like the homework first policy enforced by her parents, what were the positive effects of the author obeying her parents' policy? Do you think a homework first policy is important for parents to enforce with every child? Should there be exceptions to the rule?
2. What are possible consequences to laziness?
3. What does the Bible say about being lazy?
4. What is the opposite of laziness?
5. What does the Bible say about being diligent?
6. What are the benefits to being diligent with exercising?
7. What are the three reasons the author found in Scripture for working?

## Give Generously

"Yes, they are greedy dogs Which never have enough, And they are shepherds Who cannot understand; They all look to their own way, Every one for his own gain, From his own territory" (Isaiah 56:11).

What is God's perspective on greed? "For the wicked boasts of his heart's desire; He blesses the greedy and renounces the Lord" (Psalm 10:3). Obviously, greed is a sin.

What are the consequences to being greedy? The first by-product of greed I found in the Scriptures is great sorrow: "Woe to him who covets evil gain for his house, That he may set his nest on high, That he may be delivered from the power of disaster!" (Habakkuk 2:9). Greed also brings on God's wrath, unfruitfulness, want, trouble in one's family and society's disapproval. However, I think the greatest loss to being greedy would be being a part of God's Kingdom.

Being greedy is one of the ways man disobeys God. Thus, resulting in God's punishment. "Let no one deceive you with empty words, for because of these things the wrath of God comes upon the sons of disobedience" (Ephesians 5:6). This reminds me of how parents punish children for being selfish with their toys.

How can we display the fruit of the Holy Spirit whenever we become greedy? Christ said, "and the cares of this world, the deceitfulness of riches, and the desires of other things entering in choke the word, and it becomes unfruitful" (Mark 4:19). Greed cannot be a part of an authentic Christian's life. This vice does not mix with love, joy, peace, longsuffering, gentleness, goodness, faith, meekness and temperance.

I have heard and read stories of misers who lost everything in an instant. House fires, car wrecks, major medical problems and business deals gone bad wipe out people's bank accounts every day. "He who oppresses the poor to increase his riches, And he who gives to the rich, will surely come to poverty" (Proverbs 22:16).

Have you asked someone to loan you an ink pen or something else you might need momentarily? If they said "no", how did you react? "The people will curse him who withholds grain, But blessing will be on the head of him who sells it" (Proverbs 11:26). Thus, I believe greediness or selfishness can be classified as a social sin; besides, being sinful in God's eyes.

Obviously, individuals closest to a person more concerned over accumulating material possessions than with spiritual or intellectual goals will be affected negatively. Proverbs 15:27 says "He who is greedy for gain troubles his own house, . . ." An example might be when a greedy individual becomes a workaholic. Through the workaholism, the individual neglects his family, possibly resulting in a divorce from the spouse. Children of workaholics also can feel neglected. Even worse, the child can learn greediness from the parent.

Missing out on God's best without the previously listed potential by-products of being greedy is enough for me to want to avoid this unhealthy behavior. Inheriting God's kingdom is impossible for the greedy, according to I Corinthians 6:9-10:

> Do you not know that the unrighteous will not inherit the kingdom of God? Do not be deceived. Neither fornicators, nor idolators, nor adulterers, nor homosexuals, nor sodomites, nor thieves, nor covetous, nor drunkards, nor revilers, nor extortioners will inherit the kingdom of God.

What are alternatives to being greedy? Learning to be content is one solution to overcoming a problem with greed. Why should a person be content? I found three reasons in the Scriptures. The first reason deals with the longevity of material items. According to I John 2:16-17,

> For all that is in the world--the lust of the flesh, the lust of the eyes, and the pride of life--is not of the Father but is of the world. And the world is passing away, and the lust of it; but he who does the will of God abides forever.

A second reason to learn contentment is because "For we brought nothing into this world, and it is certain we can carry nothing out" (I Timothy 6:7). What happened to John D. Rockefeller's millions? Did he take it with him to eternity whenever he died? Have you known of anyone taking personal possessions with them to eternity?

The greatest reason I believe for being content is God's promise for provision: "Let your conduct be without covetousness; be content with such things as you have. For He Himself has said, 'I will never leave you nor forsake you'" (Hebrews 13:5).

Whenever I am in God's will and trusting in God's Word, I am never left in need. For example, I remember a time when through prayer a need was met.

"Pam, what are we going to do about food?" my temporary roommate said. "I need to eat."

"I'm sorry," I said. I looked at the dangerously obese woman across the room. I thought, *I don't think missing a meal or two will hurt either one of us.* I looked at my left ankle in a cast. "Maybe the storm will quit soon. Then I can go across the street to my neighbors' to use the telephone. I can't go out in my cast with the rain pouring so much."

"I'm hungry. I have to eat to take medication."

"All I can tell you to do is pray. There's nothing I can do about getting any food," I said as I prayed to myself, "Lord, would you please send Diane or someone here? I can't do anything about this situation."

Within a short period of time, what do you think happened? Someone knocked on the door. I maneuvered to open the door with the use of my crutches.

"Jim, I'm so glad you're here." A friend stood in the doorway holding an umbrella. I smiled at him.

"Diane is in the car," Jim said. "She wanted to see if you need anything."

"That's awesome! I just prayed that God would send one of you here. We need groceries."

"We'll go get them for you."

"Have Diane come inside while I get my money and make a list for you."

"No problem." Jim motioned for Diane to come inside.

"Diane, you won't believe," I said. "I just prayed that the Lord would send you here."

"That's awesome," Diane said. "I was sitting at home without any plans when I felt a nudging to come here to see if you needed anything."

"God sure answered my prayer," I said to my friends later whenever they returned with groceries.

"He sure did that," both Jim and Diane said smiling and nodding in agreement.

"But whoever has this world's good, and sees his brother in need, and shuts up his heart from him, how does the love of God abide in him" (I John 3:17)? Jim and Diane displayed God's love referred to in this verse.

What are the Biblical principles on giving? "You reap what you sow," I have heard so many ministers preach from the pulpit. This point comes from II Corinthians 9:6: "But this I say: He who sows sparingly will also reap sparingly; and he who sows bountifully will also reap bountifully." Verse 7 of the same chapter in the Bible instructs us to give as every man "purposes in his heart, not grudgingly, or of necessity; for God loves a cheerful giver".

Whenever we help less fortunate individuals, we need to be careful not to let pride creep into our hearts. Giving to gain recognition is contrary to the Scriptures, according to Matthew, chapter 6, verse 1 through verse 4. These verses instruct us to give to the poor secretly.

How does one break a bondage to greed? Besides the obvious prayer and repentance required to overcome any sin, I offer four additional suggestions: focus on God's Word; walk in love; give thanks; and, stay away from other greedy people.

> Do not lay up for yourselves treasures on earth, where moth and rust destroy and where thieves break in and steal; but lay up for yourselves treasures in heaven, where neither

moth nor rust destroys and where thieves do not break in and steal. (Matthew 6:19)

I suggest that a person trying to break a bondage to greed stay away from greedy individuals for two reasons. First of all, Christians are to "have no fellowship with the unfruitful works of darkness, but rather expose them" (Ephesians 5:11). Secondly, Christians are to flee evil, according to II Corinthians 6:17. Personally, whenever I spend any substantial amount of time with another person, I am tempted to let that person's habits and attitudes rub off on me. How about you?

In concluding this chapter, I want to challenge you to look around in your family and community. Ask: Who needs help? Do I have resources to help them? Lend a hand or give a gift to someone today.

## Simple Acts of Kindness

Volunteer to cut grass.

Clean a senior citizen's house.

Help a friend paint.

Cook someone a meal.

Visit a nursing home.

Help a child with homework.

## Questions for Reflection

1. What is God's perspective on greed?
2. What might be negative consequences to being greedy?
3. What are the fruit of the Holy Spirit?
4. How can a greedy person's family be hurt?
5. What are the biblical principles on giving?
6. What three reasons did the author find in Scripture to learn contentment?
7. How does the author recommend an individual break a bondage to greed?

# Fail not to Forgive

"I'm sorry. I forgot." These words were commonly heard when I lived in my parent's home years ago. Between my chemical imbalance and my parents' getting older, we got a lot of practice at forgiving. Someone forgetting to turn off a light or someone forgetting to switch the TV/VCR control back to television after watching a video was not unheard of when I lived with my parents. For example, on one occasion:

"Pam, you left the video in the VCR." My father opened the bedroom door as I was writing the first edition to this book.

"I did!?" I said surprised at his interruption. "I'm sorry."

"Yes, I've been running around here trying to figure out why the television was playing so fuzzy. It was set on VCR."

"I'm sorry. I got distracted and forgot." I turned back to my work. My father closed the door. The matter was over.

Life today living with my husband faces similar challenges as living with my aging parents did years ago. We are often reminding each other of our forgetfulness. For example, as I am writing my husband just mentioned that I forgot and left the bathroom heater running with the door opened last night. Meanwhile, this morning he forgot to complete paperwork that I needed for an upcoming doctor's appointment. My husband Milton made the comment, "I guess we're even."

"Pam, you're your worst enemy. Don't be so hard on yourself. Forgive yourself." For years I heard these words said to me by more than one friend in reference to my wallowing in self-pity over past mistakes. I had a difficult time forgiving myself of mistakes, or failures. Perfectionists are that way!

Whether we are offended at another person or disappointed at something in ourselves, forgiveness is not optional in a Christian's life. Christ said, "For if you forgive men their trespasses, your heavenly Father will also forgive you. But if you do not forgive men their trespasses, neither will your Father forgive your trespasses" (Matthew 6:14-15).

Suppose someone cuts you off in traffic. How do you respond? With anger. Is your anger righteous? Or are you swearing through your teeth? No one likes to be abused by another individual. However, we need to face the truth: abuse, injustices and mistakes happen everyday in everyone's life. What is the Biblical approach to responding to such occurrences?

One way to respond to a shortcoming, whether another individual's or our own, is to not make a big deal out of the matter. Who knows? Maybe that person who cut you off was transporting a critically ill person to the emergency room. Or maybe the driver was a doctor or a firefighter responding to an emergency page. Can you blame them for rushing? How would you have responded in the same situation?

"The discretion of a man makes him slow to anger, And his glory is to overlook a transgression" (Proverbs 19:11). Blowing off an incident where a stranger cuts me off in traffic is not a problem. After all, since the person does not know me, his action probably has nothing to do with me. That is simple enough! But what about that parent, spouse or co-worker we see stumble everyday? How often are we to forgive? Christ warned us:

> Take heed to yourselves. If your brother sins against you, rebuke him; and if he repents, forgive him. And if he sins against you seven times in a day, and seven times in a day returns to you, saying, 'I repent,' you shall forgive him. (Luke 17:3-4)

What is God's perspective on how we should treat our enemies? Christ answered that question.

> But love your enemies, do good, and lend, hoping for nothing in return; and your reward will be great, and you will be sons of the Most High. For He is kind to the unthankful and evil. Therefore be merciful, just as your Father also is merciful. Judge not, and you shall not be

judged. Condemn not, and you shall not be condemned. Forgive, and you will be forgiven. (Luke 6:35-37)

"I don't get mad, I get even", a slogan I have read on T-shirts, bumper stickers and in books. Is this approach to responding to others' offenses Biblical? Let's look at Romans 12:19: "Beloved, do not avenge yourselves, but rather give place to wrath; for it is written, 'Vengeance is Mine; I will repay,' says the Lord." Obviously, God will see that people reap what they sow.

Unforgiveness is a sin. Just as with covetousness and other sins discussed in this book, unforgiveness can leave a person in bondage. Not only a person, but entire families! For example, I have heard of family feuds lasting for years where family members did not even know what started the feud. Somewhere along the line, two individuals had a problem. One, or maybe both persons, got mad. The anger became unforgiveness; the unforgiveness became bitterness. Then through the family grapevines the entire family of both parties became riled. How pleased is God when this happens?

Have you ever rebuked someone for an offensive behavior to have him or her continue the behavior? I will share two alternatives to responding to this occurrence, through two personal examples. First, I recall a woman I used to be friends with several years ago. This lady had a bad habit of calling me to whine about uncontrollable matters. She also oftentimes ended up gossiping before she hung up. The relationship disturbed me. How did I respond? Over time I backed off from the woman, ultimately ending the friendship. There is nothing wrong with removing yourself from a situation that is abusive or unhealthy.

More recently, I confronted some women about their use of profanity at the workplace. Whenever they failed to comply with my request for them to clean up their conversations, what did I do? First, I forgave them because I realized their noncompliance might have been a matter of "old habits die hard". Secondly, I prayed for God to remove me from that setting. He sure answered that prayer! Or I would not be sitting here writing today!

"You can't control another person's behavior; but what you can control is how you respond to the person's behavior. You make the choice." . . . A key point I recall several therapists saying to me.

Forgiveness is a choice. Is there anyone you need to forgive?

## Questions for Reflection

1. Is forgiveness an option in a Christian's life? Why or why not?
2. What is God's perspective on how we are to treat our enemies?
3. "I don't get mad, I get even" is a common slogan in today's world. Is this slogan biblical?
4. What are ways the author suggests to responding to other people's shortcomings?
5. When one becomes angry and unforgiving, what is one possible outcome mentioned by the author? Are there others?
6. Do you think it's ever okay to end relationships? What example did the author give of her ending a friendship?
7. You can't control another person's attitude or behavior. What can you control?

## More Than a Grandmother

"If you want to have friends you have to show yourself friendly," Mama Owens said these words to me a lot in my younger days. She always said these words came from the Bible, but I did not learn the exact Scripture Proverbs 18:24 until I was older. Reading and discovering these words in Scripture for myself gave my grandmother's wise advice more meaning. She also quoted the second half of Proverbs 18:24: "there is a friend who sticks closer than a brother".

What impresses me the most about my grandmother's biblical advice is that not only did she encourage me to be friendly and considerate of everyone's feelings but she also set an example by being one of my closest friends for over two decades. Her friendship helped mold me into the Christian I am now. Without her encouragement and personal mentoring, I doubt that I would have turned out as well grounded as a Christian as I am today.

Mama had become widowed before my birth. Her only child was my father. During my pre-school years Mama lived in an old farmhouse across the street from my family. With this close proximity and with the very nature of our relationship as her only granddaughter, she and I developed a special bond quickly. She always said, "You're the daughter I could never have myself".

After my family moved to another part of town, Mama and I still maintained and nurtured our relationship at every available opportunity. I remember our long talks lying across her bed whenever I stayed overnight at her home. I could discuss anything with Mama, from my petty childhood problems to my biggest dreams of being a grown woman with a family and a career. During these discussions, Mama emphasized the important role Christ played in her life, and encouraged me to be the best possible person I knew to be by following the biblical principles.

Throughout my childhood and teenage years, Mama always made me feel special as she tried not to make a difference between her two grandchildren. If one of us had a birthday, both of us received a present. If she accompanied my family on a trip in the car, she always sat between my brother and me to prevent an argument from erupting over who would sit by her.

My grandmother's presence gave an additional glow to our home each holiday. I will never forget the tasty dishes she prepared for those special occasions. Her best and most requested dinner was chicken and dumplings with all the trimmings. She taught me how to make homemade dumplings, which I now fix for my husband using her recipe as she used to do for my grandfather.

As I reflect on all the turning points in my life, memories of my grandmother always surface. Her presence will always be remembered and can still be felt when I see her photo that sits on a shelf in my home. She helped me to overcome many obstacles, from my toddler years to my college graduation. The secrets we kept of how she helped me in my struggles are neither few nor far between but are lodged in my heart forever.

Like God's love, Mama's love was unconditional. She loved me through both the successes and failures of life. Sure, we had problems. But we worked through our difficulties and differences or we left them alone, not allowing petty things to destroy our special bond.

Even though my career forced me to relocate miles away from my grandmother and death later came to her, our bond remains intact in memories and through our relationships with our best friend, the Lord Jesus Christ.

Written January 1992<br>
Revised January 2016

## Questions for Reflection

1. What circumstances led to the author and her grandmother having such a close bond?
2. How did the author's grandmother influence her for the better?
3. What was the author's grandmother's advice for her to be the best person she could be?
4. Why do you think it was important for the author's grandmother not to make a difference in her grandchildren?
5. How do you think the author's bond with her grandmother remains intact today?
6. Psalm 103:17 says "But the mercy of the LORD [is] from everlasting to everlasting on those who fear Him, and His righteousness to children's children". Do you think this verse applies to the relationship between the author and her grandmother?
7. How does the Bible say widowed grandmothers should be treated? (See 1 Timothy 5:3-8.)

## A Marriage Made in Heaven
### *Milton J. and Pamela K. Orgeron*

"If a marriage isn't made in Heaven, then it's not worth the paper it was written on," Pam recalls Mama Owens telling her many times. Undoubtedly, Milton's and Pam's meeting and marriage were orchestrated by God. Here's their story:

In spite of having been a victim of sexual abuse and an abusive marriage scam, since early elementary school Pam had wanted and prayed for a Christian marriage where her husband and she could work in the ministry together. God answered Pam's prayer through Milton, who after hearing her life story, said to her, "I am surprised that you have anything to do with anyone with a "Y" chromosome after all you have been through." Here are the events leading to Milton's and Pam's marriage:

After Pam completed her Education Specialist (Ed.S.) degree from Morehead State University in Kentucky spring 2009 she could not find employment locally. This led her to look for opportunities in the Nashville, TN area. Pam had lived there from 1986 until 2000 when she relocated to Kentucky, her birth state, for graduate school. Late summer 2009 Pam moved back to Nashville under the pretense of having a position counseling women in recovery from alcohol and drug abuse at a retreat center. The position also was to include housing and transportation. After arriving in Nashville, Pam learned that the offer was a scam. When she refused to work with the individual trying to scam her, she ended up at the local women's shelter in a very unhealthy environment.

She and Milton met at Nashville First Church of the Nazarene where Pam could walk from the women's mission. Right away Milton and Pam knew God was up to something with them. Within two weeks Milton asked Pam to be his wife. She accepted.

Milton believes that Pam has been God's wonderful sweet surprise to him in many ways. He was surprised she was still alive

# Lessons Learned from Life's Realities 115

after the horrific abuse in her past. "Many people become bitter atheists when they do survive, and many abused women hate all men. But Pam's faith in Jesus is always strong and trusting and I have never been loved by anyone on earth more than by her," Milton wrote.

God works all things, even terrible things, to the good for those that love Him and are called to His purposes (Romans 8:28). He used Pam's trials and Milton's ex-wife's 12 years of refusal to work with him toward reconciliation to refine them by fire. Their struggles taught them separately to lean entirely on Jesus rather than on their personal understanding. They learned to trust Him with whatever He willed to make of their lives, which prepared them for a marriage founded on the solid Rock. From their tears turned over to Him, Jesus grew a sweet garden of a new life together. Their home and hearts joined together are filled with the peace, patience, joy and love that can come only from the indwelling Holy Spirit, never from mere human goodness. As Pam has often said, neither of them is perfect, but Jesus has made them perfect for each other.

Milton told the Lord once that he could not hope to find a wife who loved Jesus more than she could ever love him and who knew that he must do the same, and who knew that would be the best foundation for a lasting marriage. *Anyone like that must already be happily married*, he thought. But the Lord had just such a sweet woman in mind. Milton wrote, "I am forever amazed and grateful to Him for bringing us together and to Pam for being that godly, loving wife!" Both look forward eagerly to how He will use them together in the years ahead for His glory and to bring lost souls (as they once were) to His joyful kingdom!

Know a single seeking a soul mate? Someone who desires a spouse who will love him or her with the love of the Lord Jesus Christ? If so, this person needs to make sure that God is first place in his or her life, and that God knows that. A single person who desires a godly Christian marriage should apply 2 Corinthians 6:14 to living: "14. Do not be unequally yoked together with unbelievers. For what fellowship has righteousness with lawlessness? And what communion has light with darkness?" That means if someone wants a Christian marriage, that person must be a Christian first and foremost, and then be sure before dating anyone that the person also is a Christian.

Years ago a relative told Pam, "Be the right person, and you will find the right person". Additionally, Pam counsels single individuals that if they don't want to be married to someone who drinks, smokes, cusses, whatever they find repulsive, then they should not date or habitually hang out with those individuals who do what they find unappealing.

Milton and Pam believe the biggest key to acquiring and maintaining a strong Christian marriage is letting go and letting God. When a person completely surrenders to God, and leaves finding a soul mate and changing any imperfections in a current or prospective spouse to God, that person too can have a Christ-filled relationship with a home full of love and peace that only comes from the Father above.

## Questions for Reflection

1. What was Pam's grandmother's advice regarding marriage?
2. Who do Pam and Milton credit with bringing them together?
3. Why was Milton surprised that Pam risked being in a new relationship?
4. How did God use Pam's and Milton's previous trials to strengthen their marriage?
5. What advice do Pam and Milton have for singles wanting to be married?
6. What does the advice "Be the right person, and you will find the right person" mean to you?
7. What do Pam and Milton believe is the biggest key to acquiring and maintaining a strong Christian marriage?

## Maintaining Christian Character Costs

"There's a cost to being a Christian," my late father and ordained United Baptist minister Harry M. Owens said a lot. "People think they can get saved, and then go do what they want to do. That type of thinking is contrary to the Scriptures."

". . .these people who profess Christianity on Sunday, and then go out drinking and partying the next week," my father said. "There's something wrong. You need to be able to see a change, a difference in a Christian's life."

"Miss Goody Two Shoes," my classmates nicknamed me in school. This resulted from my making better grades than everyone else, and from my refusing to participate in behaviors like cheating on exams or getting involved with drugs and alcohol. I could have chosen to slack off of my studies and to compromise my beliefs to be more like the others. But, would I have been better off had I chosen to follow the world's path? I do not believe so.

Sure, I might have had more friends or been more popular in some ways by succumbing to peer pressure. But, on the other hand, I would not have the peace and satisfaction I have now knowing I stood strong and worked hard to do my best. The long-range benefits of following Christ and not the crowd far surpass any temporary advantages I might have received otherwise.

Following Christ requires submitting one's time, energy and control to God's authority. Maintaining a Christ-like character does not mean always being the wealthiest financially in your crowd; always socializing with the well-dressed, popular crowd; or, always being liked by others. Few Christians I know could win a popularity contest with the world. Christians who walk the closest to the Lord often receive the most criticism.

While writing the first edition and this edition of *The ABC's of Life for Children and Adults: Short Stories, Essays, and Poems Promoting Christian Concepts*, I purposely saved this chapter as the last non-fiction chapter to write. Why? Because maintaining

Christian character involves everything else discussed previously. I want to encourage each person reading this book to pursue holiness. I want to remind Christians:

> Or do you not know that your body is the temple of the Holy Spirit who is in you, whom you have from God, and you are not your own? For you were bought at a price; therefore glorify God in your body and in your spirit, which are Gods. (I Corinthians 6:19-20)

As Christians, we are commanded to hold the light of Christ up to the world. If we fail to take care of our mind, our body and our spirit, how can we be obedient? When I am tired or stressed from lack of sleep, unhealthy eating or no exercise, I cannot give God's best in Christian service. Can you?

Spending time alone each day talking with God is essential to maintaining peace in my spiritual walk. Through prayer, Bible reading and listening to the Spirit's still, small voice, I draw closer to God. "Draw near to God and He will draw near to you" (James 4:8).

If you want to let Christ's light shine through you, be careful whom you allow to become your closest friends. None of my closest friends smoke, drink alcohol or use profanity. I look for friends who display the fruit of the Spirit. I encourage you to be fruit inspectors in selecting your closest friends.

> Beware of false prophets, who come to you in sheep's clothing, but inwardly they are ravenous wolves. You will know them by their fruits. Do men gather grapes from thornbushes or figs from thistles? Even so, every good tree bears good fruit, but a bad tree bears bad fruit. A good tree cannot bear bad fruit, nor can a bad tree bear good fruit. (Matthew 7:15-18)

We are known by the company we keep. Remember, "Birds of a feather flock together". Much truth lies in that old saying. I encourage you to choose your friends wisely.

To the lost soul reading this book, my prayers are with you. I urge you to find a Bible-believing church where the Gospel is preached. Make your peace with God. Then seek God's direction in your life. My primary purpose in writing this book is not to witness to the lost soul but to encourage Christians to get on fire for the Lord. "No one can serve two masters; for either he will hate the one and love the other; or else he will be loyal to the one and despise the other. You cannot serve God and mammon" (Matthew 6:24).

I see too many people wearing the "Christian" label who can talk the talk; but, they are not walking the walk. For example, the community where I lived as a child was small, dry and going to a bar or nightclub was not an option. After I moved to Nashville, I had to reassess my lifestyle to determine whether I would follow the crowd, or the Scriptures. Whenever other singles calling themselves "Christians" started inviting me to go to bars, I presented a question to Dr. Seton Tomyn, then singles minister at Two Rivers Baptist Church, Nashville:

"Seton, is it okay for Christians to go to bars and night clubs, even if you're not drinking or not there to pick someone up?"

"Whenever people ask me that question, I tell them 'no', for two reasons," Seton said. "First, for Christians to go to bars is wrong because of the appearance of evil. The Scriptures tell us to avoid the appearance of evil. Most of what goes on at bars is wrong. The second reason I tell Christians to avoid places like bars and nightclubs is to avoid being a stumbling block to someone else."

To the Christian, before concluding this chapter I want to add Matthew 5:14-16:

> You are the light of the world. A city that is set on a hill cannot be hidden. Nor do they light a lamp and put it under a basket, but on a lampstand, and it gives light to all who are in the house. Let your light so shine before men, that they may see your good works and glorify your Father in heaven

## Questions for Reflection

1. The author's father, an ordained minister, said, "People think they can get saved, and then go do what they want to do. That type of thinking is contrary to the Scriptures." Do you agree with the author's father? Why or why not?
2. What does following Christ require?
3. What does the Bible say about holiness? (See Leviticus 11:44 and 1 Peter 1:15-16.)
4. What are the characteristics of holiness? (See Psalm 15:1-5.)
5. How can we give God's best in Christian service?
6. What was the author's primary purpose in writing this book? Why?
7. The author asked a former pastor, "is it okay for Christians to go to bars and night clubs, even if you're not drinking or not there to pick someone up?" What was the pastor's reply?

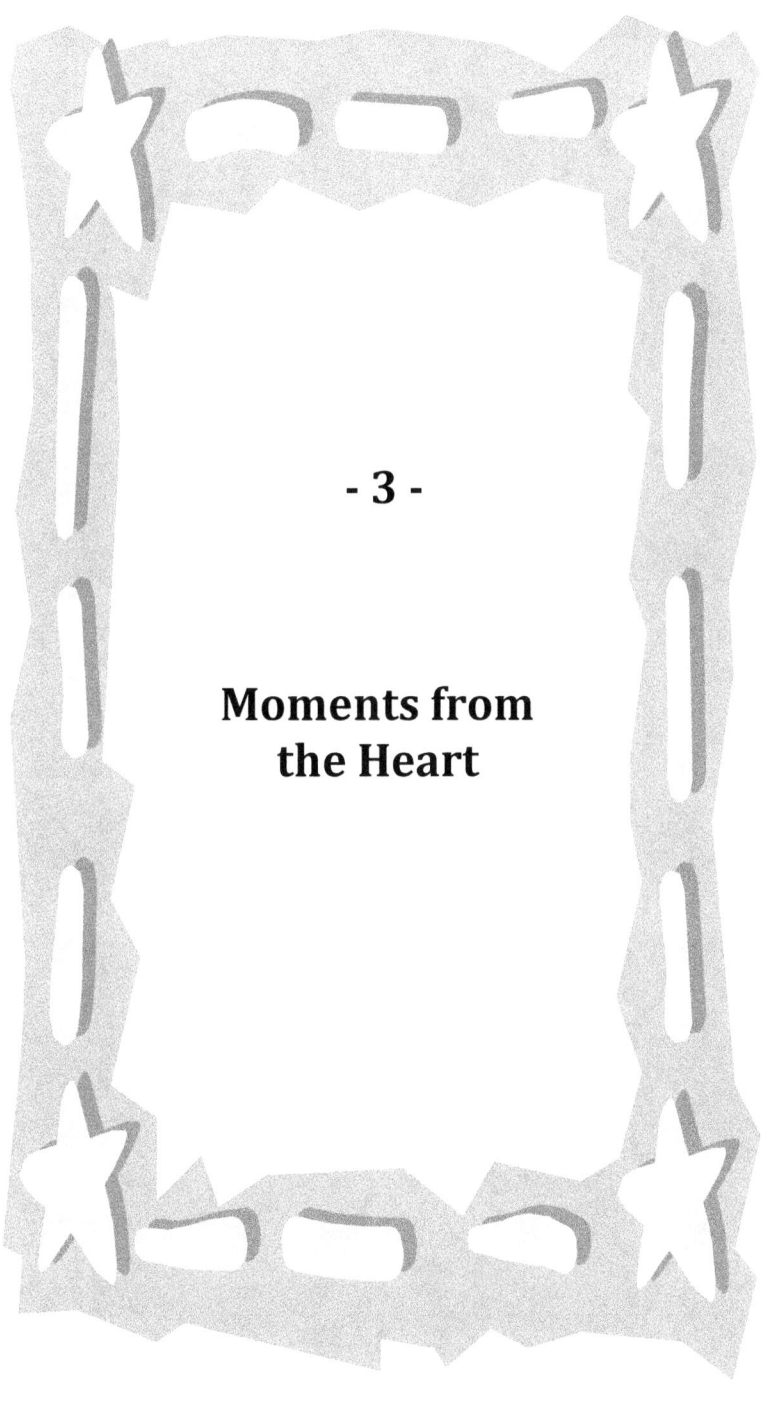

- 3 -

**Moments from the Heart**

# Complete Works of Pamela K. Owens, Volume One*

Unchanging Love
No Better Friend
Turned Around
Let the Son Shine
Channel of Blessings
Trials with Triumph
Bright and Morning Star
Heaven's Highway
In the Name of Jesus
Bless Us to be a Blessing

\* © 1993

# Unchanging Love

VERSE 1
You were with me for my first breathe of wind.
You were with me when I felt at wit's end.
Through each milestone You helped me.
This is what I want to bestow.

CHORUS
Unchanging love, unchanging love . . .
The love that never wavers---God's unchanging love.
Unending devotion, everlasting commitment . . .
Steadfast for eternity.
That's God's unchanging love.

VERSE 2
Now I feel your presence in all I do.
In both good and bad times I lean on You.
I know with You there is no fear
As I plan on future years.

VERSE 3
I long for the day when I leave this world.
Then Satan will not bother me any more.
All life's secrets will unfold
With many a beauty to behold.

REPEAT CHORUS

TAG
Steadfast for eternity.
That's God's unchanging love.
Unchanging love, unchanging love,
Unchanging love, unchanging love . . .

> "Jesus Christ is the same yesterday, today, and forever."
>
> **Hebrews 13:8**

Unchanging Love, by Pamela Kaye Owens, © 1988

# No Better Friend

VERSE 1
I remember what granny used to say.
The Lord will be your best friend.
You can go to Him any time of day.
He's a confidant on whom I depend.

CHORUS
When trials and triumphs come, I walk close to God alone.
There's no better friend.
There's no greater treasure . . .
God's grace forgives my sin and knows no end.
With God's amour from Heaven---
There's no closer comrade . . .

VERSE 2
Whether problems arise or blessings flow
I go to God in prayer.
There's so many answers I don't know.
But with God's companionship I have no care.

REPEAT CHORUS TWICE

TAG
With God's amour from Heaven---
There's no closer comrade . . .

> "... But there is a friend who sticks closer than a brother."
>
> **Proverbs 18:24**

# Turned Around

VERSE 1
I tried hard to hide behind a false face.
But You knew my heart was in the wrong place.
You let me think I was right for a while.
But You turned me around with troubles and trials.

CHORUS
Lord, You turned me around.  Yes, You turned me around.
You gave me freedom with everlasting love.
Such a sweet peace I have now since You turned me around.

VERSE 2
In Your time You showed me I was lost.
In Your way You turned me to the Cross.
I felt so filthy deep within my soul.
But You turned my life around and made me whole.

REPEAT CHORUS

VERSE 3
Since You turned me around, I feel so free.
I cherish each moment I spend on my knees.
You promise to bless me abundantly
When I depend on Your guidance faithfully.

REPEAT CHORUS

BRIDGE
Lord, I long to obey Your will since I came Your way.
But sometimes I stray.  It's then You love me anyway.

REPEAT CHORUS

TAG
Such a sweet peace I have now since You turned me around.

> "I have surely heard Ephraim
> bemoaning himself:
> You have chastised me and
> I was chastised,
> Like an untrained bull;
> Restore me, and I will return,
> For You are the Lord my God."
>
> **Jeremiah 31:18**

Turned Around, by Pamela Kaye Owens, © 1988

# Let the Son Shine

VERSE 1
At Calvary I found freedom from my sins.
Peace and joy filled my soul as I was born again.
Now this is my prayer to God from my heart.
May the lost be found before they depart.

CHORUS
Let the Son shine through me.
Kindle me to stay in Your perfect beam.
May Your light project from me.
Lord, make me a blessing aglow with Your love.
Lord, make me a blessing aglow with Your love.

VERSE 2
Show me how to be a light to the lost.
Help me remember to daily count the cost.
Let Your light shine through me in all I do.
May I never hinder anyone from coming to You.

VERSE 3
Lord, increase my faith to have to share.
May others see in me someone who really cares.
Let the Son shine from deep within my heart.
Help me encourage others to make a fresh start.

REPEAT CHORUS

TAG
Lord, make me a blessing aglow with Your love.

> "I have come as a light into the world, that whoever believes in Me should not abide in darkness."
>
> **John 12:46**

# Channel of Blessings

VERSE 1
I can turn on my television set.
I can see what this world has that I can get.
There's lots of things offered to me.
But these mundane treasures are overshadowed by what I desire to be.

CHORUS
Let me be a channel of blessings to be used by the Lord.
I'll turn off the world view and turn on to God's ways any day.
Lord, I pray, bless me now to be a channel of blessings.
Bless me now with love unending.

VERSE 2
I watch as the world streams past so fast.
I wonder how much longer can mankind last.
Sin's glitter draws both the unsaved and Christians away from the Cross.
But I aspire to reflect Jesus and Jesus only to the lost.

REPEAT CHORUS

BRIDGE
I see we need a world-wide revival,
How many people need to turn to their Bibles
And how few people choose to surrender to God's ways.
Yes, we must be living in the last days.

REPEAT CHORUS

# Trials with Triumph

VERSE 1
With mountain tops high and valleys low
Many Christians learn wisdom as they grow old.
While on the mountain others learn greed
Forgetting God's love as the ultimate need.

CHORUS
Heaven or hell's path . . . One you must choose.
I pray Heaven's treasures you won't loose.
Life on earth offers trials and triumph for you,
But will be worth the toil as God gives you life anew.

VERSE 2
Down in the valley man sinks so low
Forgetting all blessings God has to bestow.
Hunger and pain encompass our world
While Christians, full and fed, sit lazily and bored.

REPEAT CHORUS

VERSE 3
Pain and injustice spread fear through our land.
Yet few men choose to join the Heavenly band.
When will mankind awaken to see?
The answer is to be what God wants him to be.

REPEAT CHORUS TWICE

TAG
Yes, it will be worth the toil as God gives you life anew.

# Bright and Morning Star
## *(In memory of the late Keith Whitley)*

VERSE 1
My childhood dreams were to be a celebrity.
I was encouraged when I saw cousin Keith on TV.
Yet Keith was called home about four years ago.
This message I believe he would want you to know.

CHORUS
Jesus, my friend and guide, is the brightest star I know.
He's the only star in Heaven.  His Word says so.
Yes, Jesus is the bright and morning star.
His light leads the way to a better tomorrow.

VERSE 2
I've met plenty of award winners in my life.
Many of which worked so hard to see jobs done just right.
But after death how much will these rewards be worth?
No more than the poorest man's treasures here on earth.

VERSE 3
You may have more awards and fans than anyone else on earth.
But some day these trophies and bodies will return to the dirt.
If you don't know Jesus as Lord and Savior,
Then you won't get to Heaven for good behavior.

REPEAT CHORUS

Keith Whitley
July 1, 1954—May 9, 1989

# Heaven's Highway

VERSE 1
Once I enter Heaven's race,
No more tears will stain my face.
While on earth I must abide
With God's Word as my only guide.

CHORUS
Heaven's highway here on earth is rough and straight
But will be worth the cost when I enter that Pearly gate.
Troubles and sorrows will all be over
When I pass through Heaven's door.

VERSE 2
Detours will always tempt my way
As Satan's lies lead me astray.
But I must push Satan aside
As I seek a celestial ride.

REPEAT CHORUS

VERSE 3
As an impure child in God's fold
Sometimes my witness grows cold.
With faith I must move at God's pace
Until I reach Heaven's domain.

REPEAT CHORUS TWICE

TAG
Oh, when I pass through Heaven's door.

# In the Name of Jesus

VERSE 1
Look around . . . What do you see?
There's a world full of sin and agony.
I need not look far to perceive . . .
People need to trust more in Calvary . . .

CHORUS
In the name of Jesus. In the name of the Lord.
His Word is sharper than any two-edged sword.
Just call on Jesus. He's always there.
He'll heal your heart. Just kneel in prayer.

VERSE 2
Look inside . . . What do you see?
Is your heart pure white or black as it can be?
Deep inside God's voice is calling you.
Follow His call. He'll give you life anew.

REPEAT CHORUS

VERSE 3
Just call on Jesus. He'll help you too.
Just like all my trials that He brought me through.
Your broken heart He'll make brand new.
Look to Jesus! This is what He'll do.

REPEAT CHORUS TWICE

TAG
Oh, He'll heal your heart. Just kneel in prayer.

# Bless Us to be a Blessing

VERSE 1
Many years we lived looking for the right one.
We lived trusting You'd send that person our way.
Then as we had hoped You sent this anointed love.
That's why we stand before this altar today.

CHORUS
Bless us to be a blessing to one another.
Bless us to be a blessing to the world.
Bless us as we commit our hearts as one forever.
Bless us, Lord, to be a blessing to the world.

VERSE 2
We don't know everything You have planned for us.
We leave our future in Your strong loving hand.
We so desire to let Your light shine through us.
Please use us to spread Your Word across the land.

REPEAT CHORUS

TAG
Bless us, Lord, to be a blessing to the world.

# Tributes to Loved Ones

# In Memory of My Beloved Grandparents Harry and Earl Smith Owens

Mama's love meant so much.
No one else had her touch.
Papa died before I was born.
Although this loss I still mourn.

"He was my very best friend,"
Mama used to tell me.
She longed for life's end
When she'd go be with him.

Through Mama's eyes I knew him.
So much I missed never seeing him.
Mama said, "how crazy he would've been over you."
Oh, how I wish he'd lived to see me too.

Words to describe are hard to find
Of my grandmother who was so kind.
Never did she let me down.
In her a friend I always found.

With Christ in both Mama and Papa's hearts
To Heaven's country they've both now departed.
But time will never erase
Memories of their blessed familiar faces.

Written December, 1992 by Pamela K. Owens

My grandparents Harry Hermond Owens and Earl Smith Owens pictured above married August 15, 1931. They were married 28 years before my grandfather's death in 1959. My father was their only child.

## In Memory of My Beloved Parents
## Dave and Emma Whitley Sturgill

When a little child growing up
There were eleven children of us.
We were poor and didn't have much
But, oh, the love our parents gave us.

Our parents were Christians of Baptist faith.
Daddy preached from place to place.
Now we hear of revivals he'd hold,
How sinners flocked to pray for their soul.

There were many times friends came by.
They had church until way in the night.
It was praying, singing and shouting too
Like old time Christians love to do.

There were many things they taught us.
Now we cherish it all so much.
They taught us of Jesus who died on the Cross
So that no one would always be lost.

Their prayers have been answered one by one,
How they rejoiced as each one would come.
Out of eleven ten have confessed.
Now we pray for the last one left.

The old home place is remodeled and new.
But we can remember all they went through.
Now we can tell all and joyfully say
They both live in Heaven on this Christmas Day.

Written December 1992 by Patricia Sturgill Owens

My grandparents James David Sturgill and Emma Whitley Sturgill pictured above married March 22, 1919. They were married 54 years before my grandfather's death in 1973. Emma Whitley Sturgill died March 8, 1979. Their children include sons, John W. (Bill), Wilbur Garland, Paul Jack, Harold Joe, Garland, James D., and Everett G. (Jerry) Sturgill; daughters, Neva, Helen, Patty, and Sandra.

## In Memory of My Sister and Brother
## Helen Sturgill Moore and Jim Sturgill

Loved ones, we want the world to know
The happiness you brought while here below.
A friend you were until the end.
Always on you we could depend.

Brother and sister, we want all to know
The love we shared through the heat and cold.
It's this time of year we miss you most.
The tears we shed no one knows.

We all know and can feel it too
You're so happy with Jesus whom you knew.
How do we know this to be true?
We felt the love when you prayed through.

Never a doubt do we have now
Concerning your soul and whereabouts.
So rest on until that blessed morn
When all Christians will be called Home.

Written December, 1992 by Patricia Sturgill Owens

Pictured above are Helen Moore and Jim Sturgill. Most of the Sturgill family loved to camp back then. Not me! I preferred my own bed! Still do! Thank you!

Pictured left to right are siblings Jim Sturgill, Patty Owens, Neva Conley, and Garland Sturgill.

## In Memory of a Special Aunt
## Helen Sturgill Moore

I used to visit Aunt Helen a lot.
She'd always have something cooking in a pot.
Helen was one of the best cooks around.
None like her could be found anywhere else in town.

Aunt Helen also had a friendly ear,
And how she loved to spread holiday cheer.
She only cleaned houses to make a living,
But a meager living didn't keep her from giving.

Aunt Helen was easy to talk to.
I'd sometimes visit her when I felt blue.
She'd always have the right words to say,
Or whatever it took to brighten my day.

I will always remember Helen's sweet touch.
She is missed by one and all so much.
But I know she is in a better place,
Now a part of the Heavenly race.

Sadly missed by niece,
Pamela K. Owens
Written July 2, 2003

My aunt Helen Rose Sturgill Moore is missed mostly during the holiday season. Every Christmas she enjoyed decorating her home and giving homemade gifts, such as creamed candy, Apple Butter cookies, and other tasty treats.

## In Memory of a Dear Cousin
## Emma Lee Moore McGlone

Sweet Emma Lee was like a big sister to me.
I still remember her favorite nickname for me—Miss Pammie.
Sweet Lee to me was a role model like none other,
Just as was Aunt Helen, Sweet Lee's mother.

Sweet Lee had her share of problems
But she seemed to try hard to solve them.
In Sweet Lee a friend I always found,
Even when she had reason to be down.

Sweet Lee used to live in a trailer park
Where I visited for our talks, heart to heart.
She encouraged me when I went to Tennessee.
I still have one of the letters she wrote me.

I was never so surprised
To hear Sweet Lee had taken her Heavenly ride.
Now she's rejoicing with our Lord,
Receiving her just reward.

Sadly missed by cousin,
Pamela K. Owens
Written July 2, 2003

Pictured below:
Helen Moore, Pam Owens, and Emma McGlone

**"Unless the Lord builds the house,
they labor in vain who build it; . . ."**

**Psalm 127:1**

## In Memory of a Dear Uncle
## John William Sturgill

I remember visiting Uncle Bill.
He just lived over the hill.
With his backyard adjacent to Aunt Helen's
He was such a jolly, fine fellow.

Of Uncle Bill, my brother has a special memory,
How Uncle Bill performed his wedding ceremony.
I too hoped he would officiate my special day,
But a few years back Uncle Bill's heart gave way.

Uncle Bill was so humble, never one to cause trouble.
He was the oldest of my seven uncles,
Always wise and patient in his ways
Until he left for his final resting place.

Uncle Bill had three children of his own.
Each of them now has kids that are grown.
So swiftly time has passed away.
How we look forward to seeing Bill on our Homecoming Day.

Written September 2002 by Pamela K. Owens

My uncle Bill was an ordained Baptist preacher. Like most good Baptists, he loved to eat. This photo was taken at his home at a New Year's Eve Party, December 31, 1980.

## Forty One Years

Forty one years have come and gone
Since you and I were wed.
We've had our ups and downs,
But still we're looking ahead.

The children are now gone.
Now we're here left alone.
But in our hearts they still remain,
Our little children just the same.

As we walk the road of life
With its valleys deep and wide,
As we meet troubles and strife,
God's dear hand will guide.

As we live our life on earth
May my love show forth
As a rose with beauty rare
Which says that I still care.

As we walk down life's highway
And our journey's end is near,
My love grows stronger every day
And each and every year.

Patty—Thanks for putting up with me for forty one years.
Also your patience—strength—courage and love.

Your husband Marvin

Written April 29, 1996 by Harry Marvin Owens

Married April 29, 1955, Harry Marvin Owens and Patricia Sturgill Owens pictured above had two children: my brother Patrick Marvin Owens from Ohio and me. My father passed away after I completed the first version of this book. Mom still resides in Russell, Kentucky.

## The King's Highway

Well, Lord, here I am.
Take my troubles in the palm of Your Hand.
Though my burdens are great, and problems many,
If You'd only speak the word Lord, I wouldn't have any.

I've been in the valley, and I've been on the mountain.
I've been chastised, but also drank from the fountain.
My eyes are on the heavenly shore,
Following the tracks, of my Savior before.

They lead to the Father's heavenly throne,
And with Jesus my guide, I'm never alone.
He leads me along the heavenly way,
And gives me strength and courage, to finish the day.

Though Satan offers the world each day,
I have chosen to travel The King's highway.
It leads me to my heavenly home,
Where I can thank my Lord, and never more roam.

Written July 16, 1994 by Harry Marvin Owens

## **From Darkness to Light**

I was walking alone enjoying the pleasures of life,
When a door opened before me, and I walked in.
I was in total darkness, and could not see.
I said, Lord, what's happened to me.

Then I heard a sweet voice call out my name.
It said, "Child, it's the Lord. Be not ashamed.
I've come to help you and show you the way,
So you can live with me, forever some day".

Never had I felt like this before.
I thought I did not have a friend in the world.
My family and friends were no pleasure to me,
Not even my loving companion and children so sweet.

I took hold of His Spirit and followed along,
Not telling anyone what was wrong.
We travelled together for almost a year.
Then it was known, but I didn't care.

I became so sick and burdened down.
I didn't want anything, or to run around.
My house work got behind, but I didn't care.
I was lost, and had so much fear.

Then the night came when I went to church,
With no one knowing I was hurting so much.
It was the best thing I ever did in my life
Because the Lord saved me, and now I see the Light.

Written August 29, 1994 by Patricia Sturgill Owens

# Such Precious Moments
## *(In memory of spiritual birthday, 10/16/63)*

I would love for all to know
I'm not the same as I was years ago.
The Lord reached down in '63.
He made a Christian out of me.

Now, I feel you can plainly see
I'm so happy He came to me.
Then, two days later it came to pass,
He saved my dear husband, at last.

My dear husband was happy and free.
Then, the Lord spoke again, "Child, go preach."
He is preaching to all and wants them to know
Jesus died on the cross for sins, long ago.

Now, we are walking together, hand in hand.
We are on our way to the Promised Land.
Can you say that you are going too?
Don't miss out. I will look for you.

Written October 7, 1992 by Patricia Sturgill Owens

## Peaceful Shores

Not a ship or dolphin did I see
Just waves and sand and a palm tree
Little children playing in the sand
Others wading with Mom in hand.

Birds making their gentle soar,
While underneath the waves did roar.
The ocean's sound and the gentle breeze
Puts my wearied mind at ease.

It makes me long for that heavenly shore
Where the Son will be the light forever more.
No more sorrow, no more pain,
But heaven's glory will be our gain.

We'll be walking the streets of gold
Viewing the things that were left untold,
Thanking the Lord for what He has done,
And for the crown that we have won.

Written May 27, 1994 at Myrtle Beach, South Carolina
by Harry Marvin Owens

# Against the Odds:
# The Author's Personal Testimony

"If people only knew the damage they did whenever they molest someone, especially a child, they'd never do it. They'd never do it!" Elaine Baker, PhD, who was my professor of Human Sexuality at Marshall University, Huntington, WV, said (1984).

Little did I realize the significance of Dr. Baker's statement to my life until years later whenever I realized I had been a victim of early childhood sexual abuse. Maintaining healthy relationships had always been difficult for me. I could not understand why until I broke through denial and chose to take the long road to recovery.

If a person would have asked me over 25 years ago at my high school graduation about my childhood, I would have said I came from a "normal" family. I grew up living with my parents and one brother. As far back as I could remember, we attended church most Sundays. Furthermore, as a "star" student headed for college, I avoided falling into the vices of alcohol, drugs, and promiscuity.

After completing my undergraduate work in journalism in 1986, I moved to Nashville, Tennessee where I quickly found employment. In 1987 I acquired a position with the Jean and Alexander Heard Library on the campus of Vanderbilt University. At that point I had a good job, a car, my own apartment in a nice neighborhood, and I had made Two Rivers Baptist Church, Nashville my church home. What more could I have wanted?

The pivotal day as an adult that changed my life forever came about a year later—June 26, 1988, the day I crushed my left ankle. After the ankle injury, I developed symptoms of depression but was resistant to seeking help until another defining moment in my life—the day of my cousin Keith Whitley's funeral. At the time of Keith's death, I was feeling exceptionally low, even to the point of contemplating suicide.

"If you have a problem...It doesn't have to be alcohol and drugs...any problem, whether it's alcohol, drugs, psychological, or emotional, get help," said Ricky Skaggs, country music artist during Keith's funeral. "Don't let this happen to you. I know this is what Keith would want me to say."

The above words spoken by Ricky penetrated deep into my soul. Shortly after the funeral, I sought professional help. Doctors diagnosed me with Major Depressive Disorder, Anxiety Disorder, and Codependency. The diagnosis lead to months of prescription medications, psychotherapy, and journaling. In therapy, I realized my "normal" childhood wasn't normal after all.

For years from the time I was in Dr. Baker's psychology class I had suspected sexual abuse was a part of my past but my early childhood memories contained a lot of memory lapses. Based on John 8:32, I knew that I could find freedom and healing only in learning the truth about what memories were suppressed. I prayed, and asked God to show me. Bits and pieces through backflashes and journaling I dealt with what I had to in order to find peace.

Since I was first diagnosed with the chemical imbalance in 1989, the road to recovery has contained many ups and downs. I began questioning God but later realized what had happened to me was all a bigger part of His plan for my life. This realization did not come before two suicide attempts and several instances of seeing where God had used me to minister to others going through similar situations. After years of therapy, after reading all the Christian self-help books I could find, and after finding peace in spite of the past abuse and current financial and other health problems, I decided to return to college to study psychology which would better enable me to understand and to move to deeper levels of recovery. Studying the issues in counseling and psychology did in deed take me to deeper levels of healing, and I anticipate more growth in the future as I plan to pursue a doctorate in counseling psychology.

The advice I offer to anyone who suspects past abuse in his/her life—deal with it. Don't live in denial and misery all your life. Forgiveness is vital in the healing process. Many sexually abused Christians enter into a quick "forgive and forget" mode before working through their emotions and allowing ultimate healing of the heart. Before a person can offer forgiveness, an injury and its pain must first be acknowledged, for in light of the cross, there is no difference between the abused and the abuser.

Confronting an abuser can be a legitimate step in recovery if the purpose is not revenge. Sometimes direct confrontation is not possible. The aggressor may be dead or whereabouts unknown. At other times, direct confrontation is unwarranted if the person will react negatively in a way that would cause more problems. In such cases, unresolved issues are resolved through internally adjusting thoughts and attitudes. I know I wrote a lot of letters to offending persons which were never mailed.

After a person who has been sexually abused works through the recovery process, expressing concern and empathy to others provides additional hope. God wants overcomers to comfort others with the comfort they received from Him (2 Corinthians, 1:4). This is why I share my story—to give hope to the hopeless. No one has to remain a victim forever. By searching the heart and by learning to be one's authentic self, any victim can become a victor through Christ Jesus.

*Pamela K. Owens* (2003)

# Twelve Years Later: A New Perspective

Over the past twelve plus years since the first edition of this book, much has changed in my life. I have experienced both heartache and pleasure in my walk with God. I no longer see life from the perspective of a single college student. Marriage changes people; at least my marrying Milton has changed me. Often singles get wrapped up in self, and how they can help themselves more. I was one of those. Now I am more other centered, next to keeping God my first love. I also am working on focusing more on the present moment, rather than regretting past mistakes or living in a future that may or may not come. I was reminded in a sermon this past Sunday evening of 2 Corinthians 4:17--"For our light and momentary troubles are achieving for us an eternal glory that far outweighs them all." This is true.

Living in this secular world today is not easy, and often has many challenges with obstacles to overcome. One thing is sure and certain; the more intentional a person is about living for God, the more Satan attacks that person. But I realize based on 2 Corinthians 4:17 that anything Satan puts in our path or that God allows us to endure is nothing in comparison to the big picture and the peace and joy that we will find in Heaven. Not only is my insight based on Scripture, but on a personal experience where the Lord blessed me at a particular time to visit Heaven. I have never shared about this experience publicly because of fear of what the skeptics would say. But, now, I must share what *I know*. God is real! He loves you! And Heaven is real!

Being a Christian does not mean that one will be problem free or without uncertainty in life. Today as I write I face a lot of unknowns. I have a number of health and financial concerns facing me. That's okay though. I know God is in control and is greater than any disease, financial obligation, temptation, evil, or whatever that can come against me in this world. The same is true for anyone who trusts in Him and comes to know Him as Savior and Lord.

What's important for Christians is that we trust and live for God moment by moment letting His light shine through us to the lost souls we meet daily.

How about you? Are you saved? Have you backslidden? Walked away from God? Or never accepted Him to begin with. Whatever your situation, I hope and pray that through the words and insight shared in this book as inspired by God that you are motived to live a closer and more joy filled walk with Him.

*Pamela K. Orgeron* (2016)

# Final Reflections and Acknowledgements

The roots to the creation of this book extend back to when I was a student at Pine Acres Elementary School in Ashland, Kentucky. How I loved reading! I remember many times I would check two books out of the library only to finish reading both of them in one day. Most students visited the library once or twice a week but not me. As soon as I finished one book, I was never satisfied until I could visit the library again. I loved reading the biographies, the autobiographies, and the adventure stories kept on the library shelves. Deep down inside I knew that someday I too would be a writer.

Over the twelve years I spent as a student in the Fairview Independent School System, I had many special teachers who left lasting impressions on me. From grade school I recall how my first grade teacher Mrs. Holmes, my fourth grade teacher Mrs. Collins, and my sixth grade teacher Mrs. Layman were positive role models. Special high school teachers included former math teacher Charles Criss, and Carl Thompson, former history teacher and superintendent with Fairview schools. I could not have done as well without any of you. Thank you.

After testing the waters in the fields of banking and mathematics, I ended up studying journalism in college. Eventually I graduated with a B.A. degree from Marshall University, Huntington, West Virginia. I wish to extend many thanks to Dr. Ralph Turner, Dr. George Arnold, and the other journalism faculty members at Marshall who touched my life.

Many of the stories in this book originated when I was a student with the Institute of Children's Literature. Other stories I wrote during a two month sabbatical in the late spring and early summer of 2000. Thanks, Mom and Dad, for allowing me to have time to write!

After my writing sabbatical, I placed the manuscript on the shelf and returned to college to complete a master's degree. Many of Morehead State University's faculty, staff and student body are to be thanked for the existence of a large portion of this book.

"Don't give up on that dream. You have some good stuff there.": Words of a former academic advisor of mine, Dr. T. Ross Owen inspired me to pick up my manuscript again to investigate possible means of publication. Thanks, Ross!

In the spring of 2002 not long after Dr. Mark Schack shared with me about the special project he required for the EDUC 516 computer course I planned to take during the fall semester I knew what I wanted to do. There was the opportunity I needed to fine tune and publish my manuscript. Thank you, Dr. Schack for giving me the opportunity. Other Morehead professors who gave time, their encouragement, and/or expertise include Dr. Charles Glover, Dr. Deene Golding, Dr. James Canipe, and Dr. Lola Aagaard. I also appreciate Trevor Griffith, MSU Marketing Chief Designer, taking an interest in my project. May God bless you all!

Enough thanks cannot be given to Jennifer Little and her staff at the Multimedia Lab located in the campus library. Without their patience and guidance in helping me fine tune my skills of scanning, cropping, and inserting pictures and illustrations and of formatting the text and design of the first edition of this book, I doubt that I would have persevered to complete the first book. Many blessings to each and every one of you!

Debbie White and her staff at the MSU library computer lab back in 2003 also deserves applause for being patient with my many questions. In addition, only one spot in the computer lab was suitable for me to work where I could elevate my left leg and spread out the many books and papers needed to write this book. Oftentimes I would come to the computer lab to find another student sitting in my preferred seat. Thanks to those of you who graciously gave up that seat and moved to another location when I explained my situation.

Without the support of my spiritual brothers and sisters I would not be the individual whom I am today; thus, I would like to express thanks to each of the church families that I have been a part of over the 50 plus years of my life. To the members of the United

Baptist churches where I grew up and where my mother still attends today after Dad's passing, thank you for loving me and my family and for being positive role models to me as a child growing up. Other church families that I have been a part of in the Ashland, Kentucky area include the Community Presbyterian Church, Bellefonte and First Baptist Church, Ashland. All of you were influential in shaping my life. Thank you.

Words cannot express how grateful I am for Brother Jerry Sutton and his flock at the former Two Rivers Baptist Church, Nashville where God taught me many lessons. At many of the lowest points of my life, different ones at TRBC were there to meet my needs. A few I want to thank here individually. To Kay Barnett, who took me into her family and loved me like one of her own; to Dr. Edward L. King, who was my family physician for many years; to Allen Barnes, the attorney and friend who helped me through all the legal problems created from my marriage scam; to Jim Meyers, who was my prayer partner going through the MasterLife courses and of course to Brother Jerry, Tom King, and Seton Tomyn, who counseled and prayed me through many trials, thank you. I love you all!

During 2003 my church family broadened to include the congregation of the Morehead Church of the Nazarene. A special thanks to the former pastor, Brian Farmer, for allowing the Holy Spirit to work through him to encourage me. Thanks, Brother Brian! I really appreciate how you and your congregation accepted me with open arms.

Other church families who have influenced my path since 2003 include Wallace Memorial Baptist Church, Knoxville, TN; Lincoya Hills Baptist Church, Faith Baptist Church, and Music City Baptist Church, all in the Nashville, TN area; and what I claim as my two current church homes, Madison Church of the Nazarene (official member here) and Bible Holiness Church (We claim each other.), both in Madison, TN. I have nothing but love and respect for the pastors and congregational members who have ministered to me while at any of these churches. Thank you to each of you! You know who you are!

I would be amiss if I failed to express gratitude to my brother Patrick with whom I shared many good and bad times growing up. Although time and distance have separated us, I will always have a special spot in my heart for you and your family. I love you all, Pat!

"I really liked your book," said cousin David Gillum, from Orange County, California. "After I started reading it, I didn't put the book down until I'd finished reading all of it."

David's words above and encouragement from his late father, "Tiny" Gillum were the last straws that gave me the final bit of courage that I needed to submit the first edition of this book for publication. Thank you, David! I still miss your Dad!

My closest friends have usually been male so I especially value the few close girlfriends I have had over the years. From my senior year in high school, I remember Kay Crumpton. From my college days at Ashland Community College, Erin Lester (now Nolte) and Lisa Ramey (now Epling) stand out in my mind. Girlfriends I couldn't have made it without from Two Rivers Baptist Church in Nashville include Bobbie McGill, Dana DePena, and Angie McSpadden. During the time I lived in Morehead, KY my closest friends were my cousin Rhonda Runyon from the Nazarene church and Marilyn Weksner from New Britain, Connecticut whom I first met at Opryland. Marilyn, you especially have inspired me the way you have faced your own battles with Lupus. Today in 2016 Marilyn continues to be one of my closest confidants. Thank you, Marilyn! My heart goes out to each and every girlfriend, whether former or current, who has touched and those who continue to touch my life in ways I will never forget.

Next to God, now my greatest support comes from my husband Milton. For over the past six years Milton has been my life partner through thick and thin. We have faced many obstacles together. With our teamwork following the Lord's direction we have been able to buy a house that far surpasses what I expected this early in our marriage. Together with God's help Milton and I have turned that house into a home and a haven for the hurting. Without Milton's encouragement and other assistance now, this book would not be a reality. I do not know what God has in store for Milton's and my future: but, whatever lies in the future I look forward to walking by Milton's side as his wife until death do us part. I love you, Milton! Thank you for everything!

Ultimately, my greatest thanks are to the Lord Jesus Christ. Yes, I have had my share of hard knocks in life; but, He has been there to see me through, even during those times when I have stumbled or strayed outside of His will. He always puts me where He wants me keeping my feet on solid ground because He has a perfect plan for me as He does for each of you who has invested time or money into reading this book. May God bless each of you and may God extend His hand of mercy to bring peace and prosperity to the United States and around the world.

*Pamela K. Owens* (2003)
Revised 2016

# About the Author:

**Pamela K. Orgeron**, formerly Pamela K. Owens (1960- ) was born in Ashland, KY. In 1986 she received a B.A. degree in Journalism-Public Relations from Marshall University, Huntington, WV. Also in 1986 Ms. Owens moved to Nashville, TN where she spent over eight years employed with the Jean and Alexander Heard Library, Vanderbilt University. Before moving back to Kentucky in 2000, she also worked for Harris Publishing and Thomas Nelson Publishers. Ms. Owens received both a M.A. (2003) and an Ed.S. (2009) degree in Adult & Higher Education, Counseling Specialization from Morehead State University, Morehead, KY. Ms. Owens moved back to Nashville in 2009. Since then she has received an Advanced Diploma in Biblical Counseling from Light University and became a Board Certified Christian Counselor and an Advanced Christian Life Coach. In 2010 she married Milton J. Orgeron. She and Milton are General Partners in *ABC's* Ministries, and are active members of Madison Church of the Nazarene. Mrs. Orgeron is a certified writer with the Institute of Children's Literature, West Redding, Connecticut.

www.ingramcontent.com/pod-product-compliance
Lightning Source LLC
Chambersburg PA
CBHW071922290426
44110CB00013B/1443